The challenge of defending Britain

MANCHESTER
1824

Manchester University Press

POCKET POLITICS

SERIES EDITOR: BILL JONES

Pocket politics presents short, pithy summaries of complex topics on sociopolitical issues both in Britain and overseas. Academically sound, accessible and aimed at the interested general reader, the series will address a subject range including political ideas, economics, society, the machinery of government and international issues. Unusually, perhaps, authors are encouraged, should they choose, to offer their own conclusions rather than strive for mere academic objectivity. The series will provide stimulating intellectual access to the problems of the modern world in a user-friendly format.

Previously published
The Trump revolt   Edward Ashbee
The politics of everyday China   Neil Collins and David O'Brien
Lobbying   Wyn Grant
Power in modern Russia   Andrew Monaghan
Reform of the House of Lords   Philip Norton
Government by referendum   Matt Qvortrup
Transatlantic traumas   Stanley R. Sloan

The challenge of defending Britain

Michael Clarke

Manchester University Press

The right of Michael Clarke to be identified as the author of this work has been asserted by him in accordance with the Copyright, Designs and Patents Act 1988.

Published by Manchester University Press
Altrincham Street, Manchester M1 7JA

www.manchesteruniversitypress.co.uk

British Library Cataloguing-in-Publication Data
A catalogue record for this book is available from the British Library

ISBN   978 1526 12878 2   paperback

First published 2019

Typeset by
Servis Filmsetting Ltd, Stockport, Cheshire
Printed in Great Britain by
TJ International Ltd, Padstow

For all those men and women in uniform, past and present,
whose personal efforts make defence policy work

Contents

List of figures

Introduction: the challenge of defending Britain

IT is said that British troops always follow their officers, if only out of curiosity. That faith and curiosity is based on some confidence that their officers themselves know where they are taking the forces and what they will be asking of them when they arrive. For the decade of the 2020s there is a lot to be curious about. This is particularly so for Britain and many other countries rather like it – the 'significant second-rank' powers. The superpowers and the 'big military powers' form a small group that includes the United States, China, Russia and India. In military terms Britain falls into a larger group of 'significant second-rank powers' that includes countries such as France, Germany, Italy, Japan, Australia, South Korea, Israel and others. There are, of course, many countries with very large military establishments such as Turkey, Pakistan, Brazil or Indonesia, but they do not embody the all-round military capability of the second-rank league.

For these second rankers, in particular, the 2020s looks like a difficult decade. The big military powers are making the running as never before, and trends in world politics mean that warfare, defence and national security are being burdened with new demands and meanings that make the concept of a distinct and tangible 'defence policy' difficult to grasp – even inside governments, where different policy areas are supposed to be clear. Not only that, but defence policy carries a big emotional burden in most countries; the collective anxiety of a nation to be kept safe, the first duty of government towards its citizens, legacies of the past, and the still powerful sense of national patriotism. Not least, in a world of dizzying technological change and social transformation, it may not be obvious what a defence policy can realistically achieve. There are more than 27 million people in military forces around the world; the great majority of them not doing very much, and achieving even less. Many have deeply harmful effects on their own societies. Being in the defence forces is not a universally popular profession.

The task of defending Britain has always been challenging. Since the emergence of Britain as a modern state in the seventeenth century, threats to its existence and its lifelines have sometime been direct, in the danger of invasion or of European domination; but they have always been existential, in the sense that Britain has existed in a dangerous international neighbourhood where some degree of insecurity is a fact of life. As a significant second-rank military power, Britain's existential threats loom larger for the 2020s, partly because its 'international neighbourhood' is now much wider than its own continent, and also because modern states can be threatened, blackmailed or pressured in many non-military ways, using energy supplies, cyber power, trade access, refugee flows, social media disinformation, and many other activities that were beyond the imaginings of defence planners in a previous era.

Upon this vastly wider canvass of national security, it is often difficult to define just where 'defence' should sit and how much of the canvas it should occupy. The challenge of defending Britain requires more than a defence policy and the military forces to make it work. But those elements are nevertheless a key part of meeting the challenge. There is great uncertainty, however, over the precise roles that military forces should play in making a highly globalised, interdependent country like Britain as secure as possible. When military force is really required, nothing else will do; but when is it really required? Some countries, like India, China, Turkey or the United States, depend heavily on their military forces for security. Others, like Italy, Brazil or South Africa seem to nestle more comfortably within their own regional security networks and accept greater potential risks in relying far less on their military prowess. It is difficult to place Britain in either of these categories. Perhaps that is why national debates about British defence and security have become highly controversial and heated in the last decade. Defence will continue to be under the microscope for the foreseeable future. In a liberal democratic society this is both right and necessary. But what should the public and politicians expect to see under the microscope – and how to interpret it?

This book is written for those who want to understand how defence policy works and how it figures in the overall canvas of national security. The challenge of defending Britain in the 2020s is both direct and existential and there are no self-evidently right answers as to what Britain's overall security policy should be. But the defence element within that security policy is not so obscure that it cannot be clearly understood, even though it is normally surrounded by specialist jargon and high-technology responses. The essential anatomy of what governments call 'defence policy' is not difficult to categorise, and the six chapters that follow examine each essential element in turn. It consists of the money that is allocated to it; the equipment the armed forces have to operate; the personnel they deploy; their operational experience; their strategies for defence; and their expectations and preparations for whatever they think they will face in the future. It is a six-part anatomy that makes up the essential body of the policy. In a brief study, there is only space to describe in passing, the 'nervous system' that binds these parts together; the politics, the bureaucracy or the philosophy of national defence that drives policy forward.

The analysis presented here is not concerned with how Britain should meet the challenges of defending itself in the coming decade, or what it should do next. Readers will make their own judgements about that. Its contention, rather, is that anyone can understand and interpret British defence policy and decide for themselves on its appropriate place in the national security picture. To begin to make such judgements they only have to grasp the six biggest elements that make up the essential nature of British defence policy.

1

Money: the defence budget

THE money allocated to defence is a critical element in a country's ability to defend itself and field effective military forces. As with all policy areas, like health, education or social care, adequate resources are a prerequisite for satisfactory performance. In this case, however, headline figures for defence expenditure are also notoriously imprecise measures of military capability. Spending public money on defence is no guarantee that a country can deploy first-class armed forces. And since those armed forces are seldom used for genuine 'war-fighting' it is impossible to measure their ultimate effectiveness except in the direst of circumstances. Unlike health or education sectors, which must perform almost to their full capacity every day, defence forces, at least in peacetime, may be very busy but seldom perform to their ultimate capacity. They offer the country something more akin to an insurance policy where it is difficult to assess the costs of the policy against the benefits and reassurance it provides.

So much depends on how defence money is spent; on the combat teeth or the supporting tail of the forces, on the civilian infrastructure to support the military establishment; on personnel or equipment; on senior officers as opposed to those in the ranks; on future investment or immediate needs, and so on. Many countries get very little real fighting capacity for large defence outlays, because it is so badly spent; others manage to spend moderate amounts very efficiently to achieve their national purposes.

Moreover, headline figures for defence expenditure always carry great political symbolism. Comparisons between expenditure over time, or between defence expenditures in different countries, take on a deceptive clarity that inevitably generates comparative charts and league tables. Defence expenditure as a percentage of gross domestic product (GDP), for example, becomes a tangible political symbol of the measure of economic sacrifice a country is prepared to make for its defence forces. This shows not which countries are spending most, but how much of their national wealth they are prepared to sacrifice for the sake of their defence forces. In an alliance like the North Atlantic Treaty Organization (NATO), where twenty-nine countries of different sizes and varying prosperity commit themselves to collective defence for the common good, defence as a percentage of GDP has become the only politically relevant measure to assess the level of commitment they each make to the alliance as a whole.

Headline figures

With due regard to such caveats, however, these comparisons provide a starting point for further analysis. They illuminate the different contexts through which defence costs can be judged.

Historical trends

Britain has spent varying amounts of its national wealth on defence policy. All-out wars – total wars – are economically crippling and current British defence spending is predicated on the notion that it will not fight one for the long-foreseeable future, and perhaps never again.

In the past, however, Britain has spent vast amounts of its wealth on major wars. By 1782, after more than forty years that saw Britain fight the War of the Austrian Succession, the Seven Years War and the American War of Independence the government's public expenditure was running at almost

£30 million a year, as against incoming revenue of less than £7 million (Longford 1989: 641). And, in 1811, at the height of the Napoleonic Wars, when consolidated government accounts were published for the first time, government revenues amounted to some £69 million whereas its war expenditures came to around £45 million – plus another £35 million in interest on a spiralling national debt as governments borrowed to fund the conflict (Knight 2013: 389). In 1945 at the close of the Second World War Britain had been effectively bankrupted by the conflict. In 1944, the peak spending year of the Second World War, defence directly absorbed £90 billion (in 2015 prices), some 54% of Britain's gross national income at that time; around three-quarters of all government spending. The war had cost the country over a quarter of all its previous wealth and left its trade, manufacturing, reserves and infrastructure in ruins (Pelling 1970: 253; Kennedy 1981: 318). Even in 1947 defence was still equivalent to 16% of GDP. These were extraordinary times (Kennedy 1989: 472–6).

The mid 1950s are now regarded as times of 'normality' to act as a baseline for other long-term historical comparisons. Figure 1.1 shows the trend.

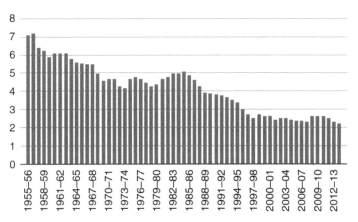

Figure 1.1   Defence expenditure as a percentage of GDP, 1955–2014

In 1955 to 1956 Britain spent 7.1% of its GDP on defence. There have been upward blips in the underlying downward trend since then, most notably during the Margaret Thatcher era of the 1980s. But it was 3.8% at the end of the Cold War in 1991 and the trend continued in a remarkably consistent way to 2013, since when defence expenditure as a proportion of GDP has hovered just above, and sometimes right on, 2% – the official target level set by NATO.

Historical trends show that enormous proportions of national wealth can be spent preparing to fight wars. Even in the early 1990s, a country such as Israel spent over 17% of its GDP on defence and still spends over 5% as its modern economy has boomed. If economies grow well, as the British economy did in the late 1950s, and again for more than a decade after 1985, even smaller proportions of GDP can still provide for a defence budget that grows in real terms.

Then too, warfare has evolved so much in recent decades that what defence pounds are spent on, and what they buy, has also changed dramatically. High-tech equipment has replaced massed armies as critical war-winners; sophisticated command, control and logistics have replaced large ammunition stocks; cyberwar and intelligence may be replacing destructive aerial bombing, and so on. In short, we might marvel at how fast peacetime defence spending has fallen as a proportion of GDP, but it is still plausible that spending a relatively small proportion of national wealth is adequate if it is spent on all the right, modern, war-winning technologies.

Current defence expenditure

In the financial year 2017–18 Britain allocated £36.0 billion to defence and plans to spend £39.7 billion by 2020–21. British defence ministers repeatedly point out that in absolute terms this ranks Britain within the top six defence spenders in the world, the largest in the European Union (EU) and the second biggest, next to the United States, in NATO (Ministry of Defence [hereafter MoD] 2017a: 8). In fact, independent league tables of defence

SIPRI, 2016[1]	
United States	611.2
China	215.7
Russia	69.2
Saudi Arabia	63.7
India	55.9
France	55.7
United Kingdom	48.3
Japan	46.1
Germany	41.1
South Korea	36.8
Italy	27.9
Australia	24.3
Brazil	22.8
UAE	22.8
Israel	17.8

IISS, 2016[2]	
United States	604.5
China	145
Russia	58.9
Saudi Arabia	56.9
United Kingdom	52.5
India	51.1
Japan	47.3
France	47.2
Germany	38.3
South Korea	33.8
Australia	24.2
Brazil	23.5
Italy	22.3
Israel	19
Iraq	18.1

NATO, 2016[3]	
USA	664
UK	56.9
France	44.1
Germany	41.5
Italy	22.3

Figure 1.2 The international defence spending league

1 Stockholm International Peace Research Institute (2017)
2 International Institute for Strategic Studies (2017)
3 Defence Expenditure of NATO Countries (2010–17), Press Communique, PR (2017) 111, 29 June 2017

expenditure do not always agree on this, since they try to create some international standardisation over what to include from official figures and use different exchange rate valuations in their comparisons. Nevertheless, as Figure 1.2 demonstrates, it is safe to say that Britain is among the significant defence spenders in the world; less than one-tenth of the US level and somewhere between one-third and one-fifth the level of China, but certainly comparable with all the other significant defence spenders.

Figure 1.3 shows defence spending in its domestic governmental context. Defence was, and remains, the fifth highest proportion of British public expenditure. The Ministry of Defence is undoubtedly one of the 'big spending' departments in Whitehall, but was allocated just over half of what was spent on education, and less than one-third of either social security or health and around one-quarter of spending on public pensions.

Composition of the defence budget

The pattern of defence spending is a critical factor in capability. The composition of Britain's defence budget reflects a longer-term trend that over the last two decades has put proportionately more into equipment than personnel.

Category of spending	% of TME*	% of GDP
Social security	29.3	12.8
Health	18.1	7.9
Education	12.6	5.5
Net debt interest payments	5.9	2.6
Defence	5.1	2.2
Public order and safety	4.2	1.9
Transport	2.8	1.2
Recreation, culture and religion	1.6	0.7
Environmental protection	1.6	0.7
Housing and amenities	1.6	0.7
Agriculture, fisheries and forestry	0.8	0.3
Enterprise and economic development	0.8	0.3
Science and technology	0.6	0.3
Other	14.8	6.5
Total	100	43.8

Figure 1.3   UK government spending by function, 2013–14

*TME = total managed expenditure, as used by HMG to represent all expenditure across the public sector from central government, local authorities and public corporations

Major Categories	% of total budget
Equipment procurement	18
Equipment running and support	24
Military and civilian personnel	33
Administration and defence estate	25
	100

Figure 1.4   Composition of the defence budget, 2016–17

During the 1990s they hovered around 39% to 40% each (MoD 1996: 47).

The total budget

Defence budgets do not account for all that may be spent on defending the nation or trying to ensure its security. Indeed, in many countries, published defence budgets are unfeasibly low, since so much is hidden in other budget lines or simply not reported. Britain, however, follows NATO's long-established guidelines in the way defence budgets should be presented.

Nevertheless, the cost of 'security' for Britain also involves defending the country from international terrorism, cyberattack, organised crime, illegal migration and disorder abroad. Other budget lines might be regarded as part of what the country pays for its security (Chalmers 2015). These are matters of judgement, but to the defence budget proper might also be added what Britain spends on its main intelligence services – MI5, MI6 and GCHQ – through the 'Single Intelligence Account'. In addition, the Home Office policing budget covers a certain amount for counter-terrorism, the UK Border Force and the National Crime Agency which concentrates on organised crime. More difficult to judge is how much of the Foreign and Commonwealth Office budget, the overseas aid budget or initiatives like the Conflict Security and Stability Fund might logically be counted as security-related expenditure.

Figure 1.5 makes some assumptions and offers an estimate for Britain's total 'defence and security budget', of over £45 billion, in 2017.

Britain's controversial 2% of GDP target

Britain has always been a loyal NATO member. In 2006 the alliance set the figure of 2% of GDP as a level that all members should spend on defence, and Britain constantly pushed to make this a reality throughout the alliance, where others were

	£ million
Defence Expenditure	36bn
Single Intelligence Account	2.2bn (covers security and intelligence agencies)
Counter terrorism spending	650m (Home Office to Met and other police forces)
National Crime Agency	430m (Home Office to NCA)
Borders and immigration	450m (Home Office budget)
Overseas aid	5bn* (of £15 billion total aid budget)
Foreign and Commonwealth Office (directly)	25m (specific security spending)
Foreign and Commonwealth Office (indirectly)	100m* (closely related security spending in £660m core budget)
Conflict Stability and Security Fund	580m (non-overseas aid portion of its £1.1 billion budget)
Total	45.435bn

Figure 1.5   Total defence and security budget, 2016–17

*Total FCO and overseas aid budgets might be regarded as making broad contributions to British security, but, here conservative assumptions are being made. Government figures include total budgets to produce an official estimate of £56 billion.

failing to meet it. Often overlooked, the '2% target' also includes a commitment that at least 20% of all defence budgets should be spent on military equipment (as opposed to pay and pensions, civilian support, and so on). Hosting the 2014 NATO summit in Wales, Britain wrote into the final communiqué a firm commitment to these targets. In 2018 only the US, Britain, Poland, Greece and Estonia met the 2% target. There is nothing intrinsically good for defence about this level of expenditure. If all twenty-nine members of NATO met the 2% target, it would add an uplift of around $100 billion to the current $250+ billion the NATO alliance spends. That may or may not be adequate for the defence of the NATO area, depending on the nature of the threats it faces at any particular time. But arbitrary as it may be, this figure takes on greater political importance than ever before, particularly in the United States where the national level is above 3.5% (House of Commons Library 2015a: 3).

British defence expenditure has been above the 2% level (and comfortably above the 20% on equipment target) since records began. But it has hovered just on the 2% level since 2014 and defence analysts have persistently questioned whether this figure can still be believed.

In accounting terms, it can certainly be believed since it conforms to NATO's criteria for what may be counted as 'defence expenditure' proper. On the other hand, NATO's criteria are quite wide and in 2015 the Ministry of Defence began to include other 'allowable' items of expenditure that it had not previously drawn into its calculations. Hence, items such as provision for war pensions, MoD civilian pensions, contributions to UN peacekeeping missions, and even some £1.4 billion of income into the MoD were taken into the equation (a grand total of over £2.8 billion). This was on top of the fact that after 2009 spending on British military operations, such as in Iraq and Afghanistan, covered by the Treasury reserve rather than from the ongoing defence budget, was also included in the NATO definition (House of Commons Defence Committee [hereafter HCDC] 2016: 6).[1] By using the full width of NATO's definitional criteria, the MoD was able honestly to say that British expenditure was still above the 2% target. In 2015 it hovered at 2.08%; in 2017 it stood at 2.14% (HCDC 2017a: Q6). On the basis of the pre-2015 definition, however, the figure would have fallen to 1.85% by 2020. Britain's GDP level in the future will, of course, alter according to the performance of the economy, but on 2016–17 trends, keeping defence just above the 2% mark would likely require over £6 billion being added to the total up to 2021. This might be covered partly by including as defence expenditure some of the budget for the intelligence agencies where they support military operations, and some future amounts from the new Joint Security Fund, from which £6.4 billion was committed to defence in 2016, spread over a seven-year period (National Audit Office [hereafter NAO] 2017: 8; House of Commons Library 2015a: 9). The latter at least, represents 'new money'.

Put simply, Britain maintains the important political symbolism of being one of the '2%ers' in NATO, though it has lost some of its moral authority in this select group by shifting the basis for its calculation. Moreover, most of the items introduced after 2015 padded out incremental reductions in mainstream military capabilities. If the accounting conventions prior to 2009 were applied in 2018, the figure would be well below 2% (IISS 2018: 72).

Persistent 'black holes' in the defence budget

Since 2015 defence ministers have repeatedly pointed out that defence spending has been increasing, both as a cash amount and in real terms (i.e. above the level of inflation). This is quite true, though the amounts are small in relation to the whole budget. A commitment in 2015 to increase defence expenditure overall by 0.5% a year in real terms; to increase the equipment part of the budget by 1% above inflation every year; and to draw some money from the Joint Security Fund, are all useful amounts at the margin and can relieve particular pressures.

The fact remains, however, that defence overcommitted itself for many years, in ordering military equipment whose arrival and servicing, of necessity, would extend for over two decades or more. Between 2011 and 2014 the government claimed to have eliminated the £30 million 'black hole' that had arisen in unfunded future commitments, but this effort was not sustained, and a number of political guarantees were then offered during the 2015 general election campaign which resulted in some £24 billion of unfunded forward commitments being made (or confirmed). In the National Security Capability Review of March 2018, the government recognised that it needed to look again for new ways to find another £2 billion every year for the next decade, to deliver the defence policy that had been agreed in 2015 (HM Government 2018: 14–15).

To get back on track the MoD built into its figures expectations of future savings through 'efficiencies' and largely relies on them to balance the books over a period. By the end of 2016 the MoD was required to find £7.3 billion in more efficiencies while it was still looking for £2.5 of earlier efficiency savings from the 2010–15 period (NAO 2017: 21–4). Of course, any big organisation can reduce costs by becoming more efficient, but when targets are so high it is easy for 'efficiencies' to become a device to build unjustified optimism into future costings, with the result that they become a euphemism for manifest (and largely unstructured) spending cuts.

While it is true that in real terms more is being spent on defence than ever before, the harsh reality is that in a high-tech world the costs of military equipment, trained personnel and digital-era support for them have risen more quickly than these budgetary increases. There are structural reasons why such demands on defence spending always tend to increase, as discussed in Chapter 2. Three Conservative-led governments after 2010 all made distinct efforts to take some pressure off the defence budget, notwithstanding the 'austerity agenda' that affected other areas of government, provoked by the decade of economic crisis that began in 2008.

Nevertheless, there are also one-off reasons why British defence spending has come under such pressure in that time. First, after a row between the Treasury and the MoD in 2007 the costs of renewing the nuclear deterrent were put directly into the defence budget. The nuclear deterrent is operated by the Royal Navy in its fleet of *Vanguard* submarines, but as the strategic deterrent force, this was previously built with 'Treasury money' – it was a national asset, not a navy one. After 2007, however, the £41 billion costs of building the *Dreadnought* successor that will replace the existing *Vanguard* force in the 2030s have been put into the main defence budget

(House of Commons Library, 2017a: 15).[2] The costs of the new *Dreadnought* programme during its peak spending years in the early 2020s easily exceed the £20 billion, decade-long shortfall identified above.

Second, as discussed in Chapter 2, around 12% of the future equipment programme is sourced abroad and is paid in dollars, and some in euros. After the Brexit vote of 2016 the value of the pound fell by more than 20% against the dollar (less against the euro). In the future it may rise again, and the MoD always factors 'currency fluctuations' into its financial forecasts. Nevertheless, sterling's effective devaluation between 2016 and 2018 was around 20% and appeared to be structural, despite a suspicion that it was then undervalued. Such persistent devaluation was certainly more than the 'fluctuations' the MoD normally anticipates.

Finally, the 2010 defence programme was built on an implicit assumption that after the immediate pain of austerity the economy would recover strongly after 2015 and the ten-year programme for defence equipment and forces pay would then be quite affordable. By 2020, it would all be back in good shape. But the economic recovery was weak after 2015 with GDP growth predictions revised downwards to 1.3% by 2020. A defence budget of 2% of (sluggish) GDP growth would be easier to achieve, but would still fall behind rises in other costs, especially those for equipment.

Is the MoD inherently different from other ministries?

The MoD is frequently criticised for being unable to manage its budget. There are, however, some unique elements that make the MoD unlike other big spending ministries in Whitehall. It has a split personality. The MoD has to be both a peacetime ministry, managing its big budgets according to Treasury rules, and also the supreme military headquarters in time of war-fighting. When British forces are on operations, the MoD must manage the process, feeding down from the military chiefs to the operational headquarters in Britain and abroad who conduct the business (Elliott 2015: 77–80).

In real military conflict there are no prizes for coming second and the need to 'win' or to 'prevail' in some meaningful way becomes paramount. There is a constant tension between the needs of the Treasury and the Cabinet Office on the one hand, who naturally require lean and efficient continuity; and the MoD and the armed forces on the other, who know that warfare is full of unique demands and nasty surprises. The spikes in demand that military conflicts provoke are normally greater and much less predictable than those made on education or housing provision or even on the Health Service in a severe winter or a global pandemic. Emergency services personnel risk life and limb in their roles, but the MoD is unique in requiring those 141,000 of its employees in uniform to be prepared to put their lives directly on the line as part of their core occupation.

None of this justifies poor planning or profligate spending, but the defence establishment is primarily charged with the first duty of government – the physical protection of its citizens. In absorbing 5% of government expenditure to do that, in an economy of some £1.9 trillion, even 'black holes' of $20 billion over the decade should be seen in the context of £2 billion a year that has to be found to deliver the planned programme. The more central question, to be addressed in later chapters, is whether the money being spent on defence is consistent with what politicians and the public think it will produce; whether the country's strategic aspirations are in line with its levels of defence expenditure.

Notes

1 The government has stated that this has been the practice since 'at least 2009' but have been unwilling to admit, even to the HCDC, exactly when this accounting practice might have begun (House of Commons Defence Committee 2016: 6).

2 Building the *Dreadnought* force is estimated at £31 billion with another £10 billion allowed as a 'contingency' amount. Running costs of the force, normally included under the core defence budget, are estimated at 6% of the annual defence budget – around £2.5 billion annually by 2020. So, over the 2030s to 2060s life of the force, running costs might be anything from £70 to £100 billion, or possibly more.

2

Kit: the military equipment

THE quantity and quality of military equipment – 'the kit' in popular military parlance – always commands press and public attention. The number of ships, tanks and aircraft that Britain fields seems more noteworthy than the weapons they carry, or the intelligence and control systems that back them up, still less the number and quality of the people who operate them. Yet as military equipment gets ever more expensive, the numbers of ships, tanks and aircraft that Britain procures has inevitably shrunk. This has created a long-standing frustration among defence commentators which has centred on two persistent complaints: that the military now have too few essential combat platforms – the 'big kit' items – to be effective, however sophisticated the next generation of weapons promises to be; and that the government has simply proved itself incapable of procuring the necessary kit effectively, without wasteful delays and chronic overspending. They are symptoms of a deeper, existential problem for a second-rank military power determined to field world-class military forces. Most military kit is not like civilian goods, which might be manufactured in mass numbers at declining real costs; it is more akin to 'tournament' goods, like Formula 1 cars, that will be used in smaller numbers in a winner-take-all competition (Davies et al. 2011: 32). It is very difficult for a mid-level military power to keep up with this. The strategic aspects of the phenomenon will be examined further in Chapter 6, but the procurement aspects are the most tangible and soak up significant amounts of public money.

The amount of major kit British forces can deploy

The low absolute numbers of major combat platforms – the ships, tanks, aircraft, and so on – that Britain can now deploy are driven essentially by cost calculations. Each new generation of combat platforms, whether on land, or in air, sea or space, self-evidently cost significantly more in real terms than the platforms they replace.[1] It may, therefore, seem surprising that there is so much uncertainty and disagreement in measuring defence equipment inflation. In his *reductio ad absurdum* in 1983 Norman Augustine famously extrapolated that by 2054 even the United States would find itself able to afford only a single, massively sophisticated and fabulously lethal new aircraft (*Economist* 2010). But more specific calculations are not easy. New generations of military equipment are normally so much more capable and potent than their predecessors that they cannot normally be regarded as a one-for-one replacement; they may be allocated quite different or more extensive missions; new types of combat platform, such as drones and robots emerge to revolutionise aspects of the battle space. Not least, the total cost of, say, a new aircraft will not be a single final figure but rather a series of fluctuating figures as it goes through research, to prototype production, full production and possibly export production (therefore with offsetting economies) across a period of thirty to forty years.

Thus it is that Britain will procure a number of new *Lightening II* fifth-generation fighter/bombers – also known as the F-35 – in a deal with Lockheed Martin of the US – a deal in which Britain is itself a partner having bought into the development and production phases – and is due eventually to procure 138 aircraft for the Royal Air Force (RAF) and the Fleet Air Arm (FAA). Under cost pressures after 2015, the government was repeatedly unwilling to confirm whether it really did plan to acquire all 138 aircraft by the 2030s. By the end of 2018, it is expected that Britain will have taken delivery of eighteen F-35s in total. Britain is receiving further aircraft at a rate of about two or three each year – and both government ministers and Lockheed executives were not unwilling, but simply *unable*, to give Parliament a firm figure for what each aircraft might cost in eight or ten years' time (HCDC 2017b: 21, 24). The first fourteen were priced differently, from £131m to £161m per aircraft, though subsequent copies may come down to around £120m each as economies of scale kick in. But the total cost per aircraft, including the particular requirements for the RAF and the FAA, is independently assessed as somewhere between £130m and £155m each, since previous batches have varied from £80m to £170m each (where one-off costs were included). This programme began, at least for Britain, in 1995 and will reach the end of its procurement cycle sometime after 2030 (Bronk 2016: 1; HCDC 2017b: 21). Long-term cost estimation is a very imprecise science.

Nevertheless, though economists may disagree over the levels of defence equipment cost inflation, there is no dispute that the phenomenon exists – that it is always higher than consumer price inflation and indeed higher than in other comparable realms of public high-tech equipment procurement (Bangert et al. 2017: 61). Some estimates are that the big British defence projects since the end of the Cold War have seen 2.2% –3.4% annual inflation; others, sampling a wider range of systems, set it as high as 8%–11% annually (Chalmers 2009; Kirkpatrick 2009). US estimates over a longer period have calculated air and maritime platform inflation as between 7% and 11% annually, depending on the particular type of aircraft or ship being analysed (Arena et al. 2006, 2008).

If one-for-one comparisons and precise costings can be elusive, every general since Alexander the Great has nevertheless understood that absolute numbers matter in conflict and that in warfare, 'quantity has a quality all of its own'.[2] The high-tech capabilities of any combat platform have to be balanced against the number that can be afforded, as well as the ease with which an adversary might negate its superior capabilities.

Ships are the most obvious type of combat platform – a single vessel from which is projected military power in many different ways. The last time British forces went to war alone was during the Falklands conflict of 1982. On that occasion the Royal Navy deployed two of its three available aircraft carriers and twenty-three of its sixty-one frigates and destroyers – the workhorse warships of a modern fleet. By 1996 Britain had two available aircraft carriers but a force of only thirty-six frigates and destroyers. In 2017, the navy commissioned a new aircraft carrier, with a second due in 2020 but had only nineteen frigates and destroyers, with question marks hanging over the future even of that number. A similar trend is evident in submarine numbers. In 1982 the navy deployed six submarines to the Falklands out of a total of twenty-six available (excluding the four submarines carrying the nuclear deterrent force). In 2018, the equivalent submarine force consisted of just seven vessels. However powerful the new generation of warships are, vessels can only be in one place at a time, and for those who worry about the decline in platform numbers, the constraints are potentially debilitating to a navy with global ambitions.

Platform numbers cannot be expressed so dramatically for air forces or armies, though the trend is the same. Airpower was critical to the Gulf War of 1991 and the Royal Air Force could choose from over thirty front-line combat squadrons to send to the operation. In 2017 it had only seven equivalent squadrons and they were at full stretch in operating in Iraq and Syria, in the Baltic States, and in providing sovereign air defence for the Falklands and the British homeland.

For the army, platform metrics are more complex. The fundamental challenge for the army is not mounting the small-scale expeditionary operations that it undertook after 1992 in the Balkans, Sierra Leone, Iraq and then Afghanistan. Its most relevant yardstick of *preparation* is instead the two short, sharp wars it fought in Kuwait in 1991 and Iraq in 2003. Most importantly, it should be assessed against a demonstrable ability to fight with NATO in a general high-tech war in Europe for collective and national defence. During the Cold War, when the army was scaled to fight for its life within NATO, it fielded 180,000 troops with commensurate armoured vehicles, artillery and tanks. Even a decade after the Cold War, it fielded some 120,000. But in 2017 it was down to 78,400 and faced further cuts by 2020. Troops use a wide variety of different combat platforms. Before the end of the

Cold War the army fielded around 900 main battle tanks – the most iconic platform for land forces – and 425 major artillery pieces. In 2018 it was planning a total force of no more than 227 tanks, and with further army reorganisations possibly as few as 170, beside no more than 250 major artillery pieces. Of course, Cold War numbers in themselves are misleading as a guide to future conflicts, but the comparison raises questions over whether the orders of magnitude involved – a 57% cut in troop numbers, a 75%–82% cut in tank numbers, a 42% cut in artillery pieces – really reflect such new dynamics of land warfare if a general conflict again became a possibility within Europe.

Perennial problems of defence contracting

The Defence Equipment and Support organisation (DE&S) of the MoD handles the bulk of contracting for all the military kit the armed forces need. Based at Abbey Wood near Bristol, the DE&S is a big organisation, traditionally employing some 18,000 civilian and military personnel, though by 2018 it had been slimmed to around 12,000.

It has to live with a record that most politicians and observers regard as unsatisfactory (Kincade 2008). Since 1992 the NAO has examined the biggest defence contracts annually and every year has pointed to systemic cost overruns and late delivery. In 1999 the NAO judged the MoD's handling of past procurement to be highly unsatisfactory (NAO 2000). Since then it has certainly noted improved procedures, but not sufficient to keep the procurement budget on track and its 2016 and 2018 reports were full of warnings (NAO 2016, 2018). By then the cost of building two new aircraft carriers had risen from less than £3 billion to £6.2 billion. The fact is that very few major defence projects are both on time and on budget.

In 1997 there was an attempt to reform contracting practices with the introduction of a 'smart procurement' initiative, which eventually ran out of steam. In 2010 there was an ambitious attempt to restructure the whole system by introducing a 'GOCO' arrangement – government owned, company operated – which would have inserted a private sector consortium as the link between the MoD and industry, and put on it all the detailed contracting requirements with manufacturers and suppliers once the MoD had specified the fundamentals of its own requirement. The consortium would then also bear the financial risk if projects went wrong. This, too, failed and by 2014 the machinery was back where it had started (*Economist* 2013). In 2015 the government took away from DE&S the responsibility for building the next-generation nuclear deterrent, creating a new Submarine Delivery Body as a separate organisation, responsible for the whole nuclear programme.[3] The DE&S was redesignated as a 'Bespoke Trading Entity' at 'arm's length' to the MoD in the midst of yet another 'transformational' management programme (DE&S 2017: 6).

Does all this represent a continuing failure of top management in DE&S, and a simple lack of contractual expertise as it negotiates with giant defence contractors? Most observers (and ex-defence ministers) would agree that it does. It is one of the perennial frustrations of Britain's defence policy. By 2018 its management had worked hard to try to get DE&S away from civil service restrictions on staffing and pay that constrained its skills in dealing squarely with major defence companies. But if DE&S's problems only concerned leadership and contractual skills, they could have been solved in the 1990s. There are some deeper structural fissures in the procurement nexus that make reform along more civilianised lines notoriously difficult.

Britain's defence procurement landscape is quite different from its civilian commercial landscape, and also significantly different from that of the United States, where the scale of military investment and production is so much greater. Successive British governments have long maintained that they take a strictly 'commercial approach' to defence procurement, relying on market forces to get best 'value for money' in all projects. But the conditions under which they operate make this an aspiration more than a reality.

With so much consolidation in defence industries over recent years and so little export potential for top-of-the-range military kit, the British defence market is largely a monopoly/monopsony; few viable suppliers and only one viable customer – the government (Heidenkamp et al. 2014). The British defence giant, BAE Systems, incorporates so many defence firms that it supplies around 40% of all Britain's defence equipment (Bangert et al. 2017: 62). Pan-European defence giants such as Airbus are part of a three-way collaboration with BAE and Italy's Finmeccanica (now rebranded Leonardo) to produce *Typhoon* aircraft for the RAF. Rolls-Royce provides the lift fan for the vertical take-off variant of Lockheed Martin's American F-35 fighter/bomber. BAE and Dassault of France jointly develop new drones, and so on. The few US and European 'defence majors' and their subsidiaries deliver the vast majority of big defence contracts.

Added to this is the highly protectionist nature of the international defence market, particularly in the US and within the EU (Uttley and Wilkinson 2016: 573–4). So, it is not surprising that the MoD has a limited list of suppliers who benefit from more than £15 billion spent on equipment every year. In a listing of its hundred top suppliers, around fourteen companies emerge as the MoD's predominant partners in a pattern that has altered little over recent years – seven of them essentially British, four mainly European and three unambiguously US companies (MoD 2017a).[4] A new monitoring organisation established in 2015 identified almost £60 million that the MoD had been overcharged across twenty big contracts that had, necessarily, been awarded on a non-competitive basis (SSRO 2016: 3).

On the other side of the equation, the major defence contractors genuinely *are* the only companies who can deliver the high-tech equipment required. Their research base is necessary to produce state-of-the art weapons platforms, they invest heavily in the early years before there is much clear profit, produce small unit numbers, and therefore enjoy few economies of scale (BAE's *Hawk* training aircraft is a notable exception in selling so well to different markets around the world). The major companies act as the 'prime' suppliers, creating consortia of necessary partners and a pyramid of contracts to the component suppliers, service companies, and so on. BAE, for example, has no fewer than 9,000 individual suppliers. Not least, such companies train and nurture the highly skilled workforces without whom high-tech equipment could not be produced at all. Major defence contracting is only for the big players; only they have the weight to live with the idiosyncratic demands of the defence procurement market.

These demands are reinforced by the dynamics of the military establishment. Military planners are naturally reluctant to risk fighting with anything less than world-class weapons systems and they cannot know which adversaries they might face over the thirty or more years that a combat platform is likely to be in service. Nor can they accept platform numbers falling below a level that would lack military credibility among allies and adversaries. The result is a conspiracy of optimism – also shared by defence companies and many politicians – that a big spending programme over thirty years *may* turn out to be fully affordable if in that time the economy does better, if the government decides to spend more on defence, if it can be produced more efficiently, or defence exports lower its production costs, and so on. There is also the fear among planners that if they drop an item they are very unlikely to get it back; lost military capabilities are far more expensive to recreate years later. Keeping all possible equipment options open over such long procurement cycles is a natural tendency for the military. Indeed, the alternative could be worse. Over a procurement cycle of twenty to thirty years it would be impossible to order *any* major combat platforms if the MoD had to be completely certain of its committed funds that far in the future. All big projects carry high levels of financial uncertainty.

They also carry big political consequences. Modern British governments have been wary of claiming to use defence expenditure to support the domestic economy. Free market ideology and the aspirations to support competitive tendering to get best value for money in defence was easy to assert, but always proved much harder to achieve (Dorman 2002: 162–3). Moreover, free market ideology made governments reluctant to embrace a strong 'defence industrial strategy' in this sector. A series of proposals have been published and tepidly followed, then replaced or rethought with changes of government (MoD 2005, 2012a; HM Government 2014; MoD 2017c). But though the defence industry accounts for only about 1% of Britain's GDP (Louth 2013: 24) it resides overwhelmingly in the high-tech/high-value sectors, employing over 160,000 people directly and over 200,000 supplying components and services to it (ADS 2014). Some 53% of defence sector jobs are in research, engineering, production or assembly and the sector also accounts for 5,000 apprenticeships (Dorman et al. 2015: 41–2). And though big combat platforms are not particularly exportable, the British defence sector still manages to earn around £10 billion annually exporting various equipment and services.

It is impossible for governments to ignore these attributes, or to be oblivious to the regional political effects of concentrated shipbuilding facilities in Cumbria and Scotland, or aerospace around Bristol, and so on. The cancellation or curtailment of major defence projects will normally generate some toxic political fallout and in the absence of a strong, longstanding defence industrial strategy, short-term political calculations tend to overshadow defence policy proper. This is one of the structural weaknesses of the system that, at least, could be addressed relatively easily by more resolute political leadership.

The ten-year equipment programme

In 2017 the government confirmed that it had allocated a total of £178 billion to defence equipment and its necessary support over the decade from 2016 to 2026. It allocated around £15 billion of it during 2017, rising to a maximum of £19 billion during 2025, before tailing off a little in the final year of the period (MoD 2017d: 4).

Of that £178 billion total, £105.4 billion (59.1% of it) is allocated to new defence equipment and immediate support for it; £67.2 billion (37.7%) to ongoing support for equipment already in service and £5.25 billion (2.9%) is held as a contingency reserve (MoD 2017d: 7). Expressed differently, £82 billion will be spent on equipment, £91 billion on support and £5 billion held as contingency (NAO 2017: 4).

The 'big ticket' items all this will fund include the second of the two new *Queen Elizabeth* class aircraft carriers and the completion of the fleet of eight Type 26 frigates, followed by five new Type 31e frigates; the completion of the seven *Astute* class attack submarines; and the start of construction of the four *Dreadnought* class nuclear weapon submarines that will eventually replace the existing *Vanguard* submarine fleet carrying the Trident nuclear deterrent. The list includes buying from the United States nine new *Poseidon* maritime patrol aircraft, more *Typhoon* fighter aircraft and the unconfirmed number of the new American *Lightening II* aircraft; more 'unmanned air systems' (drones) and new generations of air and sea defence missiles; upgrades for the Army's *Challenger II* tanks and *Warrior* fighting vehicles, alongside the purchase of a new fleet of *AJAX* armoured vehicles, the development of a completely new 'Mechanised Infantry Vehicle' and a long-overdue overhaul programme for the personal kit of individual soldiers. The ten-year plan also covers investment in the critical ISTAR technologies that will back up new command-and-control systems.[5] Not least, the plan includes investment to provide mid-life upgrades for helicopters, existing weapons, logistics chains and new tankers, patrol vessels and transport aircraft (MoD 2017d: 18–30).

The list is impressive and reinforces Britain's intention to acquire world-class military equipment; as good as any fielded by the US, Russia or China, and potentially better in some areas if it is operated with skill and guile by British forces. The MoD is determined that its forces will not lose any technical edge in the 2020s or succumb to a 'cheap and cheerful' mentality that might make front-line forces vulnerable to rapid defeat in any high-tech war-fighting.

Nevertheless, the programme also involved some significant trade-offs. As the NAO pointed out, the costs of the total programme rose by 2.1% in the previous two years (roughly consistent with inflation over that period) but then jumped by 7% in 2016 (NAO 2017: 6). To meet these increases the MoD had to squeeze other areas of future defence spending to transfer cash into the equipment programme. It had to assume that more efficiency savings could be made, both in equipment and in core MoD spending, but without specifying where these efficiencies might reside. And it had to avoid confirming precise numbers of just how many new combat aircraft it would buy or armoured vehicles it would upgrade, since these were relatively elastic elements in the plan. More uncertainty was introduced by the financial effects of the Brexit vote. Over £18 billion of the programme is paid in dollars and £2.6 billion in euros (NAO 2017: 31). If the 15%–20% fall in the value of sterling persists over the decade, then the complete programme will cost between £3 and £4 billion more by 2026.

When equipment plans come under sustained pressure defence ministries are always tempted to 'move the programme to the right', stretching delivery dates to find more time before payments are due and/or buying fewer units, or only confirming early tranches of a total order to keep open the option eventually of buying fewer units (Dorman 2002: 150–1). After 2010 the government was determined that the MoD would not again slip into this syndrome to disguise an unsustainable equipment plan. But by 2015, having made some £24.4 billion of new equipment commitments in the course of the general election and the subsequent defence review, the 2016–26 plan was clearly falling back on just this practice. In 2018 the government's audit office cast doubt on whether the MoD had ever really got its budget in order after 2010 and pointed to a ten-year deficit by 2027 of at least £5 billion, and possibly as high as £21 billion. It criticised the MoD for again allowing too much uncertainty, and optimism, into its equipment budget (NAO 2018: 7–8).

The most explicit trade-offs, however, were revealed in 2018 when the government's claim to have conducted a 'financially neutral' and 'light touch' capability review across all the elements that contribute to national security, was forced to confront far more painful and significant changes to defence plans in order to support the ten-year equipment programme that had already been significantly 'moved to the right' to remain affordable.

A 'baroque arsenal'?

Criticisms that modern defence equipment forms a 'baroque arsenal' – locked into a syndrome of vested interests that renders it overspecified, technologically racing against itself, too expensive and more cheaply neutralised – are not at all new (Kaldor 1983). But even British defence chiefs took to echoing warnings that kit that is technically 'exquisite' or which 'take years to offer 100% solutions' may not be robust enough or available in sufficient numbers to maintain military credibility (RUSI 2013, 2017).

Dramatic and rapid technical innovation resides predominantly in the globalised, civil sectors. Breath-taking innovations in computing, robotics, artificial intelligence, nanotechnologies and materials science have all occurred while the MoD was struggling to restructure its DE&S organisation. The task for the big defence companies is to synthesise these innovations and integrate them into the major weapons systems. For a significant military power, there are no easy fixes that would merely 'weaponise' civilian technologies and put them on the front line. Weapons and their platforms need to have some very specific attributes and there is no getting around the essentially idiosyncratic nature of defence procurement. Many questions therefore remain as to whether British governments can meet these challenges while trying to stick essentially to free market philosophies in a monopoly/monopsony situation; whether the biggest defence companies can really integrate what the civil sector produces; and whether anyone can spot which new innovations have a genuine potential to change the characteristics of battle over the next thirty years and perhaps force new thinking about how warfare might be conducted.

It is clear that present trends in British defence procurement are unsustainable; that the government cannot deliver its 2016–26 equipment programme, at least as it intended, on the basis of current spending and under the existing procurement regime. Moving the programme further 'to the right' would buy time but increase all the structural pressures that already make it essentially unsustainable. Other options would be to spend more on defence – in the order of £20–£40 billion over the coming decade – or to couple this up with a big push to develop those new technologies that might undermine traditional combat platforms, in effect exploring aggressively the prospect of transforming Britain into a different type of military power (Louth and Bronk 2015). This is discussed further in Chapter 6.

There may be some comfort for defence planners in the knowledge that similar pressures face all military powers. But the difference between big countries like the US, China, Russia or India, and mid-rank countries like Britain, France, Germany or Japan is in the levels of global military ambition that Britain expresses compared to them.

Notes

1 The only exception to this might turn out to be cyberspace, which, as a new domain of warfare, is only now coming to be properly assessed for its military potential and relative costs.

2 This quotation is often attributed to Joseph Stalin when discussing Soviet war strategy, though it is more likely to have originated with Vladimir Ilyich Lenin.

3 This initiative was also an explicit attempt to create a delivery body that was more like those that had delivered rail projects such as HS1 and HS2, Crossrail and also the 2012 Olympics.

4   They are, BAE Systems, Boeing, Rolls-Royce, Airbus, Lockheed Martin, Thales, Qinetiq, Leonardo, MBDA, Babcock, Serco, Capita, Atomic Weapons Establishment and Hewlett Packard.

5   ISTAR stands for intelligence, surveillance, target acquisition and reconnaissance.

3

Troops and spooks: people, intelligence and special forces

THE character of warfare constantly changes with technological and social transformation. The characteristics of twentieth-century warfare were self-evidently different to medieval warfare, and the characteristics of twenty-first-century warfare are as different again, merely fifty years later. The *nature* of warfare, however, is essentially unchanging. It involves the ability and determination of one group of fighters to impose their will over another; to kill and risk being killed in order to create the conditions for a political outcome. 'Battle' is traditionally a competition at the extreme ends of human violence and endurance, and 'warfare' is a competition between states or societies to impose their political will (Keegan 1976: 295–8).

Those who 'fight', in the broadest sense of the term, are fundamental to a functioning defence policy. Whether or not they are fighting, the anticipation that they will, if required, go to war is critical to their ability to do all the other things military personnel more usually do – acting as a deterrent to aggression, backing up civilian tasks, training and assisting other forces, engaging in foreign diplomacy, gathering intelligence, and so on. The military represents the state's greatest instrument of legal, lethal force. As the saying goes, whatever else the military do, they are ultimately trained to 'kill people and break things'.

A warrior nation

The quality of the people, popularly referred to collectively as 'troops' regardless of the colour of their uniforms, is therefore the bedrock of British defence. In 2018 there were some 141,000 British service personnel. The army constituted just over 78,400 regulars; the RAF 33,600 and the Royal Navy 29,500, of whom 7,000 were Royal Marines. These regular troops were directly supported by over 56,000 MoD civilians (MoD 2017e: 6).[1] Backing them up was a force (not all fully trained) of up to 32,000 army reservists, another 30,000 ex-regular reserves, and around 6,600 reserves for the navy and the RAF (MoD 2017f).

Thanks to the legacy of victory in two world wars and the long transition from an extensive empire, the British traditionally have an international image – and certainly a self-image – as a 'warrior nation'. British armed forces rate themselves, person for person, among the very best in the world; well trained and armed, highly disciplined, focused on getting results and accustomed to winning where it matters.

To the extent that these virtues truly exist within Britain's forces, however, it is not through some sort of innate 'Britishness', but rather because there are precise historical and cultural reasons for the public's commitment to their armed forces. There is also a political class that sees enduring value in backing diplomacy with military power and significant amounts of public money have been put into it (YouGov 2014; Beckett 2016). Above all, the armed forces are very ambitious (not true in many countries) working hard to remain a top-tier military force; preparing through training and exercises to engage in real combat operations. The motto 'train hard, fight easy' is axiomatic within British forces, and recruitment to all three services is normally highest when the forces are fighting somewhere and declines when they are not.

Nevertheless, the popular warrior image of British troops has taken some knocks in recent years. With the end of the Cold War, British forces deployed in proactive roles to Bosnia, Croatia, Macedonia, Serbia, Kosovo, Sierra Leone and Afghanistan not to mention air policing and two outright wars against Iraq in 1991 and 2003. Despite inevitable reverses, all these operations were militarily successful. British forces were winners and the public assumed they would always prevail, even if the forces performed miracles of improvisation to do so. After 2004, however, the image became more complex as operations in Iraq and then a new operation in Afghanistan dragged towards indeterminate conclusions. Air operations in Libya in 2011 and then in Iraq and Syria after 2014 proved controversial. British forces seemed to be struggling to 'prevail' in messy foreign conflicts and a trickle of allegations of misbehaviour and abuse by British troops (some true, but the great majority proving false) dented the confidence of the public in the superiority and utility of British armed forces (NatCen 2012; HCDC 2017c).

It is not unusual for there to be peaks and troughs in society's view of the military and in the military's own view of itself. Much depends on the changing international context in which Britain exists. The current context is discussed further in Chapter 5. At all times, however, there are certain constants in the relationship between the military and wider society and in the determination of military morale.

Many observers cite the history and traditions of all three armed services as something that creates an enduring military ethos. They certainly have strong traditions that are vigorously maintained; Trafalgar night for the navy, Taranto night for the FAA, Battle of Britain night for the RAF, a host of individual regimental commemorations for the Army, including Waterloo, ceremonial roles in London and annual events around Remembrance commemorations every November. But though the sense of history and tradition is undoubtedly strong, its influence on the British military ethos can be overstated. For all the public fuss when military units are threatened with abolition or merger, the degree of 'rolling change' the forces undertake is quite impressive. The keen awareness of 'tribal traditions' does not prevent front-line units being reconfigured on a regular basis as the forces seek greater combat efficiency. Army regiments have been in a 350-year state of expansion, contraction, merger and change (Mallinson 2009: 491). British forces work more 'jointly' – between all three services – than in almost any other country and their organisational evolution does not demonstrate narrow minds among military chiefs. Over the last thirty years they have shown themselves to be remarkably pragmatic. If anything, the pull of British history works more strongly on the modern public's view of the military rather than on the military's view of itself, which is notably unsentimental.

The historical ethos provides a general backdrop to Britain's military culture, but other factors are more directly relevant. The first is that Britain's armed services are predominantly volunteer, professional forces. National conscription has existed in Britain for only twenty-four of the last 350 years, in sharp contrast to the forces of most of its western partners. Britain's volunteer forces constitute about 0.4% of the adult population of Britain (less than half the corresponding 1% of US all-volunteer forces). Taking pride in being a fully professional force has been a strong driver of military morale through the last several decades. No matter that the largely conscript forces of the two world wars, unit for unit, were generally outperformed on land and air in Europe by their German enemies (Mallinson 2017; Hastings 2011: 663). With the commitment of US forces, the allies eventually overwhelmed the opposition and the warmth of victory in such titanic struggles fed an undiminished professional pride.

As a volunteer force, however, the military constantly has to compete with the attractions of employment in the domestic economy. What the military refers to as its 'offer' to service personnel has to be attractive to those who might earn more, under less stringent conditions, doing civilian jobs. It also has to compete with expectations of family life and adequate housing for troops and their families. Simple appeals to patriotism only work in times of national emergency. And though patriotism is a distinct part of the 'offer', it must be set within the development of skills and lifestyle benefits that will allow someone to live reasonably normally and enhance their civilian prospects when they leave their service. Operating in a globalised economy and within a dynamic society, the essence of the modern military offer has focused on the retention of troops more than their recruitment. Recruitment levels wax and wane as civilian unemployment goes up or down and whether or not the forces are engaged in combat operations. But the forces can normally meet recruitment shortfalls with short-term incentives to enlist. The more serious problem is in retaining personnel after they have been expensively trained. This is where the competing attractions of civilian employment have most impact on the military. To lose young, able professionals after, say, seven years in a service instead of the ten or fifteen they have ideally been trained for, is an expensive process and one that can sap the morale of a service. Around 20,000 people leave the forces every year as a matter of course. More particularly, the three services identify over eighty 'pinch point trades' where specialists in engineering, electronics, weapons handling, etc., are vital to many other military functions, and have taken extraordinary measures to keep those pinch points staffed. But many of them still showed acute shortages after 2015. The Royal Navy, in particular, lost people in many specialist maritime trades who were simply essential to sending ships to sea, which in late 2017 proved a breaking point that kept most of its nineteen-strong frigate and destroyer fleet in port.

In 2018 the services were facing some acute retention problems. Expectations of family life and career plans for the partners of service personnel, housing and educational opportunities for children, even levels of fitness and obesity across British society, created what former defence minister Mark Francois described as 'a perfect storm'. It was harder for the services to compete with civilian life. After Iraq and Afghanistan unmarried people were less inclined to enlist; but the tempo of 'operational work' under pressures of successive cuts made more experienced, married personnel more inclined to leave early. It created, he said, 'a continuing process of hollowing out' within the forces that was likely to get worse rather than better (Francois 2017: 2–3). Certainly, the official 2017 figures were stark. Personnel shortfalls normally vary greatly between the three services, depending on operations and broader demographic trends. During the

Afghanistan campaign in 2006 the Army was 1.8% down on its full establishment, while the navy was 3.6% short and the RAF 4.4%. During 2017, however, the navy and the RAF were around 10% down on their annual recruitment targets to achieve their full establishment and the Army more than 30% short of its 2016–17 recruitment target (NAO 2006: 1–2; Francois 2017: 2).

The second key factor is the psychological relationship between the British public and its armed forces. It has varied greatly over the years, from scepticism and indifference to warm respect and affection. Such recent affection reached a peak during the second Afghan campaign beginning in 2006 – Britain's fourth Afghan War – and veered somewhat towards indifference after 2015 once the combat forces had withdrawn and the political inquests began about interventions in far-off campaigns.

Recent years have also seen an interesting development in the relationship between the public and the military. Only in 1998 did a defence review, for the first time, explicitly include a 'policy for people' chapter. For all the centrality of personnel in military effectiveness, previous reviews had never addressed it as a key issue. The MoD understood, however, that it was competing more fiercely with the civilian world for the people it needed, and the forces had already been busy in peacekeeping operations in former Yugoslavia. This caused the army to rewrite its military doctrine and a phrase coined by the writers that there was an implicit 'military covenant' between the people and its armed forces caught the imagination of politicians and the press alike. Most service personnel had never heard of anything resembling it, but Prime Minister Tony Blair said the 'military covenant' should be 'renewed', and for the popular press it immediately became an 'ancient pledge' that certainly existed in the time of Wellington's army – all completely untrue (Dannatt 2016: 310–11). Nevertheless, it was recognised in law in the Armed Forces Act of 2011 and it now serves as a (non-binding) standard by which all three branches of the military, in return for the singular nature of their service, are entitled to expect support and fair treatment from public bodies and due respect from the public (Ingham 2014). It serves as a banner for opposition politicians to wave at the government when they want to champion the treatment of service men and women.

The third enduring factor lies in the very nature of the task itself; what it is to undertake a military profession. As with all professions (but more so in this case), the attractions range from noble to entirely selfish. And they seem to exist in a confusing mixture of the two for most individuals. Many senior officers are frankly proud of the fact that they have saved many lives by choosing to threaten, or take, others. They have protected the weak, and they have helped keep the country safe and free by being prepared to make the ultimate sacrifice themselves. The forces are very clear that they serve 'Britain', through their personal oaths to the monarch; and not its government, even though they take their orders from it. But personal motivations are also mixed with less lofty ambitions. Many young men and women long to test themselves in the most extreme circumstances; many want excitement and danger; some explicitly want to 'go to war'; some are attracted to the challenging existence or the glamour of the uniform. Others see the forces as a route to technical skills for which they would otherwise struggle to qualify.

Above all, the camaraderie within the forces is a fundamental element in what makes a military career different to almost anything in civil society and which can create unrivalled fighting morale. In warfare, troops fight for a hierarchy of personal motives. They fight for a 'cause' that they may or may not understand. Above that, they fight for Britain because they have been sent by the country they pledged to serve. Above that again, they fight for the honour of their service and their unit within it, understanding that thread of history which gives them pride in their cap badge or shoulder flash. But a long way above all this, they 'fight for their mates'. When British troops operate in small groups inside larger formations, they maintain astonishing cohesion and courage in the face of all challenges. In most conflicts, unit cohesion – whether in ships, air squadrons or ground formations – is the difference between victory and defeat

(Keegan 1976: 52–4). When individuals are separated or have to operate on their own they are without the natural moral support that tends to keep them disciplined and courageous (Moore 2009: 114–23).

The British military has long understood the special importance of small unit identity in both war and peace. The regiment and battalion, the squadron or the ship are family units in every sense, building on the mutual dependence between individuals but also uniting their own families and the rest of the service in a close support network. It is one of the most enduring characteristics of the British military and increasingly separates it from more individualistic occupational trends in post-modern society. Not least, for those who have lived it, there is an alluring freedom for military personnel in the conflict zone; freedom from civilian bureaucracy, freedom to improvise, to enjoy uproarious black humour, and freedom to concentrate only on their deadly teamwork. Danger and fear are great personal levellers.

Even within the conflict zone, however, British forces are required at all times to act legally. British service personnel remain subject to UK law whether they are at home or fighting abroad. In any battle zone so designated by the government, different rules apply but all troops are nevertheless subject to them. This has become more contentious in recent years. In 2003 the Chief of Defence Staff (CDS) insisted that the government had to provide a written assurance that an invasion of Iraq was legal before he was prepared to order British forces to undertake it. More recent cases of legally questionable behaviour in the battle zone and ambiguity over whether killer drones could be used outside a defined battle zone have proved difficult for both ministers and military chiefs. They have insisted that all breaches of UK law or the laws of armed conflict must be clearly punished. But they have also struggled with a natural instinct to support their troops operating in no-war-no-peace grey zones where policemen and friends in the morning can literally become guerrillas and terrorists in the afternoon. The strengthening of human rights law, and its application in conflict areas, has added more sensitivity to the way armed forces are required to act. In reality, there is no evidence that military personnel are acting under any greater legal restraint than fifty years ago, though there is a general perception among *them* that they are (HCDC 2013: 47–8). Since the withdrawal from Iraq in 2011 a plethora of fraudulent legal claims against the military, and a small but steady stream of credible ones, some dating back many years, have damaged the confidence of serving personnel that they will be fully supported by their superiors as they react to all the human pressures of operating in grey zone battle spaces.

Finally, and too easily overlooked, is the depth and breadth of training and exercises as a factor in military moral and effectiveness. It is axiomatic that training and exercises are vital to performance. The trick is to build flexibility and adaptation into training and exercises so that a whole military force can act organically, rather than mechanistically, and with a single tactical brain, but without losing its grip on essential skills and organisation. Britain's military can claim to be among the best handful of forces in the world that can do this. Training and exercises are also vital to the individual experience for those in uniform. Continuous training offers them the chance to widen their skills to parachuting, signals, electronics, amphibious operations, education courses, and so on. And exercises are vital, so they gain confidence in using their equipment and their command structures, stress-testing them under different conditions.

On the other hand, service personnel do not want to spend all their military careers training and exercising. They enlist to do the real thing – whether in combat or other types of operation. They overwhelmingly feel they are 'making a difference' when they go on operations, with an ever-positive mindset, even where there may be doubts about the higher strategy. But while there is no substitute for doing the real thing, it cannot be denied that operations also have a narrowing effect on trained skills levels. While *Tornado* crews were flying endless reconnaissance circles in operations over Bosnia they were not getting their low flying training or their bombing practice. While soldiers endured all the dangers of foot patrols in Northern Ireland or Afghanistan, they were not training with their artillery or armoured forces arms, or getting in some assault training. In bigger armed forces this is managed through rotation in and out of operations, but in a small military establishment more of the whole force has to be committed, more often, to any enduring operations. At their present size, Britain's armed forces can train for a wide range of skills, or they can go on operations where they will use a small selection of them. But they find it increasingly difficult to do both simultaneously.

Good training and proper exercising is expensive and therefore prone to a spending axe. Cuts here can be politically disguised since they have an insidious long-term effect but not an immediate one. Given the multinational nature of most contemporary operations, exercising with foreign military partners is even more important. Notwithstanding more recent NATO initiatives for combined and joint exercises, too much British training has been trimmed and many exercises have been diminished, delayed or cancelled since 2010. The MoD has somehow to rediscover the sweet spot in training and exercising British forces. Training has to make military service worthwhile; exercises have to be frequent and realistic enough for the troops to feel confident they are ready for operations; and they should go on real operations, but not for too long or too often – the exciting stress of operations eventually turns into exhaustion and disenchantment.

A much-discussed subject that is overstated in the morale and effectiveness of British forces is the contention that service personnel suffer disproportionate psychological damage, either from combat or simply by serving in the military at all. From 2006 a number of new military charities sprang up to supplement the roles that the Royal British Legion traditionally plays, and partly in response to this, the government made veterans affairs a specific ministerial responsibility in 2010. There are 4.5 million veterans in Britain and some of the problems they addressed were real enough after campaigns in Iraq and Afghanistan that cost the lives of 639 troops, with some 5,000 'wounded in action'. But a media perception emerged that somehow all military personnel were likely to be damaged by their different experiences. Recent research does not confirm the popular view (Wessely 2013: 205–8). It is emphatically not the case that a high proportion of homeless are ex-service personnel – the real proportion seems to be around 5% to 6% (mainly young and ex-Army) (Royal British Legion 2009). Nor is it the case that they are overly represented in the prison population – quite the opposite. Even within their own 'social class cohorts' young servicemen and women are 30% less likely to be in prison; those convicted are primarily guilty of violence or sexual offences rather than theft, fraud or dishonesty. Again, within their own social cohorts serving troops have a lower incidence of drug abuse (for which less than 0.5% are annually discharged from the military) and there is no convincing evidence that levels of marriage breakdown or antisocial behaviour are greater. They do not experience unusual levels of mental health problems while serving, or in later life. They report dramatically lower levels of post-traumatic stress disorder (PTSD) than among US forces (Shephard 2001: 392; Fear et al. 2010; Macmanus and Wessely 2013; Goodwin et al. 2015; Rona et al. 2016: 7). On the other hand, the experience of combat certainly appears to increase personal risk-taking behaviour afterwards, and this assumes many forms that are not yet properly understood (KCMHR 2010: 20–8). The Army, in particular, acknowledges that alcohol abuse among its personnel is higher than would be expected if they were civilians, alongside all the attendant problems associated with alcohol dependence (Goodwin et al. 2017). This is proving to be an ongoing challenge to British military authorities who pride themselves on their pastoral care.

The front-line forces

Though British military personnel share many common char-acteristics, they are members of three branches of the armed forces that are organised very differently. There are structural differences between them and many observers claim this also creates an inherent divergence in strategic perspectives; that they each see the world and its defence challenges differently. Certainly, there is a structural difference in their relationship to weapons platforms. The old adage is still true that the Army 'equips the man', while the Navy and the RAF 'mans the equipment'. Soldiers are fundamental to an army. They occupy ground within the battle space and deal directly with people there, whereas navies and air forces operate very sophisticated weapons platforms, sometimes a considerable distance from the battle space.

In itself, this should not make for a fundamental divergence in strategic perspectives between the services. If there are differences they appear to stem more from the fact that Britain is determined to maintain 'full-spectrum forces' even at low numbers. British forces aim to do everything that bigger, modern forces can do, albeit on a smaller scale. This instinct has two important effects. One is that in scaling what full-spectrum forces should be capable of doing, the United States sets the standard. British forces have always expended great efforts to remain technically in step with the US military and try to organise themselves so that they can fit into US battle formations. They also judge their minimum numbers and formations as the minimum the United States would take seriously in a junior partner. The second effect is that, at such small numbers, each service has to concentrate on essential tasks. They have no spare capacity and they have to make hard choices. So each of the armed services is forced to decide what its fundamental purpose should be, the very essence of its political utility to Britain. All three services have rethought their roles since 2015, reorganising themselves for a new decade around some central strategic perspectives. There is a vigorous debate over whether the answers they have each come up with are necessarily consistent (Elliott 2015).

The Royal Navy traditionally protects the waters around Britain and in the Atlantic. In the Cold War this role meant concentrating on anti-submarine warfare. In 1968 the navy also assumed the role of running the nuclear deterrent as the force became an exclusively submarine-based missile system. This was all consistent with the Royal Navy's tradition that it constitutes the principal defence for the British Isles. But for over two centuries the navy has also seen itself as a force for efficient power projection with a global reach (Till 2006: 10–11). The government's decision in 1998 to build two large aircraft carriers, both of which will be in service by 2020, was an investment in the enduring belief that Britain would always play a global, and not just a European, role (Childs 2012: 145). Large aircraft carriers are impressive pieces of military kit that can perform many roles, peaceful and warlike, anywhere in the world. They carry enormous political symbolism to engender both fear and goodwill. They are also big targets and represent a potential point of catastrophic operational failure if they are destroyed, so they need multilayered protection by sea, undersea and air. In Britain's case, with its small navy, the carriers effectively drive the force structure for the rest of the service. In peacetime, British ships can safely do many different things around the world; but in war, Britain could deploy – and protect – one powerful carrier battle group, and very little else. In peace, or in limited conflicts, 'carrier power projection' is extremely useful for those who can afford it. But, in major war, the opportunity costs are severe.

The RAF, like the navy, is a highly technocratic and specialist service, operating powerful but naturally vulnerable aircraft and drones. Regularly since the 1940s airpower has been hailed as a strategic war winner by itself. It has never proved to be so, though it has reached a degree of technological maturity that makes it extremely potent in every aspect of warfare. Dominating the air and space environment – if it can be done – is the best method of achieving ultimate military victory in any conflict. Nevertheless, the RAF, like most air forces, has felt the need constantly to justify its role as an inherently strategic weapon rather than as an arm of tactical support to ground and naval forces (Heuser 2010: 336–42). The RAF is also concerned with power projection, within Europe or anywhere else in the world, given enough refuelling tankers and friendly foreign bases. Unlike the navy, it had paid comparatively little attention to the defence of the British homeland and ever been concerned with having 'reach', and delivering 'strategic effect' in whatever it does (Peach

2003). Above all, it has been concerned with operating as great a number of world-class aircraft as possible, on the assumption that they will be flexible enough to re-role quickly as the need arises. In principle, the four purposes of an air force have changed very little over the years; to operate fighters for defence, bombers for attack, and a range of aircraft for reconnaissance and transport. Given the high costs of any wing of modern aircraft, alongside its extensive technical footprint, the RAF can only invest in so many front-line aircraft and seeks to make them as multi-role as possible. There is no doubting the technical excellence of the RAF, but questions are regularly raised as to its genuine flexibility. Operating a small 'Quick Reaction Alert' for the air defence of the UK, running *Operation Shader* against Islamic State in Iraq and Syria, contributing to anti-Russian 'air policing' over the Baltic States and defending the Falklands, left the RAF at full stretch in 2017, given the greatly reduced number of front-line squadrons it could field.

The Army, by contrast, is soldier-centric and therefore spreads its technical risks around an equipment fleet that is much larger, more diverse and individually much less expensive than ships and aircraft. In the last ten years the Royal Navy and the RAF have both effectively recapitalised themselves around the new aircraft carriers and the *Typhoon* and *Lightening II* aircraft. But the Army was last recapitalised around new armoured forces in the mid 1980s, some forty years ago, and then spent twenty of them mainly in light expeditionary operations, accumulating new equipment that was appropriate for those operations but not for more fundamental defence purposes. In 2015 the Army began a long overdue recapitalisation programme around new equipment, reshaping itself into a force explicitly structured to fight in major war, not only in expeditionary operations. The Army therefore scales itself around its ability to field a full combat division (normally upwards of 15,000 troops), centred on any three brigades, from a total of five deployable brigades – two of which would be new, fast and potent 'strike brigades'. Such a combat division can operate independently and is big and powerful enough to build in all the other support, intelligence and civilian elements to make it flexible and effective. Whereas the Army previously structured its combat elements only around brigades (some 5,000-plus troops) and could improvise them together into a fighting division, as it did in the 1991 and 2003 wars, it would now train and equip itself at divisional level for war-fighting and improvise for lesser demands – not vice versa.

Are the three services thinking in strategically divergent ways? With small forces, the Royal Navy can only create one carrier battle group, and by definition, that is for power projection beyond Europe. The battle group formation is barely appropriate to any conflict across the European continent. With small forces, the Army can only field one combat division, and that is predominantly based on the likely demands of a European conflict. It would require prodigious logistical feats to get it anywhere else in its full formation. With small forces, the RAF is stretched to provide full air cover in more than one theatre at a time, let alone war winning 'air dominance'. It all looks somewhat divergent. Of course, British forces expect to operate with allies in almost all combat circumstances and these big formations give the country something impressive to offer to any coalition. Then, too, in periods of 'fraught peace' the ability of the navy to contribute to western forces around the world while the Army reassures European allies of its preparedness, might represent an optimum strategy. Nevertheless, when full-spectrum forces are small, they fall back on fundamental war-fighting purposes, and it is difficult to avoid the conclusion that the three services anticipate different sorts of war.

The background spooks

All military forces are composed of troops and some 'heavy metal'. Increasingly, however, they have to be integrated with background spooks; the hidden forces that provide intelligence, strategic communications, electronic surveillance, jamming and a wide range of 'combat enablers' so that the troops and heavy metal can be deployed in the best ways and at the right times. For small, full-spectrum combat forces such as Britain's, they are not merely desirable, but essential. To remain world class, Britain has invested in the military spooks. Some are obvious combat enablers, others are often referred to as 'the dark side'.

The most important combat enablers in modern forces are in 'C4ISTAR' – inelegant shorthand for a wide range of technologies; Command, Control, Communications, Computing, Intelligence, Surveillance, Target Acquisition and Reconnaissance (Baverstock 2001). In principle, these are game-changing technologies running vertically and horizontally through the force structure; up and down from the radios or thermal imaging of infantry soldiers to the satellites that link into headquarters, and back and forth between units in any of the three services, and among any group of allies that find themselves operating together (Nitschke 2011: 14–21). The British programmes that do this range from the *Sentinel R1* battlefield surveillance aircraft that carry the Airborne Stand-off Radar (*ASTOR*), to surveillance drones, to laptops on the ground and headquarters computing systems that integrate the whole picture. The aspiration is to create a 'common operating picture' across the whole activity, a 'command information system' that is scalable, flexible and mobile, and a 'knowledge management' function that handles all inputs appropriately.

Of course, the reality is somewhat different to the promise. C4ISTAR technologies originate overwhelmingly in the most innovative parts of the civil sector and the military can find itself constantly chasing rainbows as it tries to harness them over long procurement cycles. In 2004, for example, the ambitious DABINETT programme was launched, intended to produce a unified architecture to direct, process and disseminate all ISTAR flows to their final users in the battle space. In 2006, its money was diverted to more urgent needs in Afghanistan; in 2008 it was broken down into three phases and in 2010/11 it was transformed into a diverse set of 'continuous assessment phase' initiatives as its money ran too short and its civil technologies too fast. Investment in C4ISTAR is a tempting target for immediate savings. The MoD plans to spend £4.6 billion on its ISTAR Operating Centre between 2016 and 2026, excluding what is being spent by the individual services on some of their own platforms and systems (MoD 2017d: 33). More indicative is the £29.8 billion that will be spent in that time by the Joint Forces Command at Northwood, established in 2012, and charged, among other things, with delivering the C4ISTAR backup for the forces. This is a 35% increase in its original 2012 budget, though around 50% of new investment in C4ISTAR will be used to upgrade in-service equipment in the next decade and around half will go into new equipment (MoD 2017d: 30).

The reality is that a single, complete (and *enduring*) C4ISTAR system is the philosopher's stone of force planners, and a country with ambitions to full-spectrum forces has little choice but to keep pursuing it. All military forces have to exist in a ubiquitous electromagnetic environment (EME) that is expected to change greatly in the coming decades and a great deal can go right – or wrong – for forces that can or cannot cope with a dynamic EME (Roberts and Payne 2016: 9–12). British military planners can at least take comfort from the fact that few other nations are currently working as hard to structure themselves around the best C4ISTAR technologies. A surprising number of other countries still see their military punch in terms of 'mass', rather than 'effect' and even Britain's European allies put much less into the exploitation of these enabling technologies. The United States, of course, is closer than anyone to using its C4ISTAR to unite all six domains of warfare – sea, subsea, air, land, space and cyber. So far, it remains in a league of its own.

The second enablers, the true spooks, reside in the intelligence agencies and the Special Forces (SF). In both areas Britain is acknowledged to have world-class 'assets' on a genuine par with the US, not merely as a junior partner. Britain's four main intelligence agencies all contribute to national security. MI6 deals with foreign intelligence, MI5 with domestic intelligence and policing, GCHQ with cyber security and monitoring, while Defence Intelligence (DI) synthesises all inputs from different intelligence branches across the services. All are charged with assisting British military forces on operations as required. The work of GCHQ and MI6 has become increasingly important to operations as they track criminals, terrorists, guerrillas, clandestine militias and warlords in the grey zone conflicts that characterise the modern world (Aldrich 2010: 532–9). Intelligence work is normally structured around the pursuit of signals intelligence (SIGINT), electronic intelligence (ELINT) and the most precious of all, human intelligence (HUMINT). Britain led the US in intelligence operations in 1945 and their collaboration became the basis of the 'Five Eyes' intelligence sharing arrangement that also includes Canada, Australia and New Zealand – the old 'anglosphere'. Anachronistic as the membership may now be, the Five Eyes remains the premier intelligence club in the world. Everyone wants to join it, but no one else can.

Closely allied with intelligence work are the darker arts of 'strategic communication'; the contest that goes on in the global information arena to set the 'narrative', control the 'images', win the 'hearts and minds' of those abroad and at home who form the bedrock of public willpower to prevail or give up (MoD 2012b). Successful strategic communication must be based on truth and reality. But representing them is not enough. They have to be packaged and presented in ways that will have timely effects on the sharp ends of any operation. And an adversary's corresponding efforts have to be neutralised. Good intelligence is vital to all this, so that strategic communication plays into its appropriate cultural context, not against it.

More tangible are the SF. They consist of the Army's Special Air Service (SAS) and the Royal Navy's Special Boat Service (SBS), formally backed up by the Special Forces Support Group, which draws primarily from the 1st Battalion the Parachute Regiment, and also includes some Royal Marine commandos and RAF Regiment specialists. The SAS also has two reservist units that regularly back up its operations, while the SBS has a reserve force of individual recruits. In recent times, SF has contributed specifically to the counter-terrorist work of the security services in Britain, and occasionally abroad, through the Special Reconnaissance Regiment (formed in 2005 from the legacy of the SF's Northern Ireland operations) alongside a new Special Signals Regiment created the same year.

The roles of the SF are less glamorous than is popularly portrayed (Morgan 2008). They characteristically operate in hostile areas doing intelligence and reconnaissance work. What makes them 'special' is their ability to operate in very small groups, or individually, and to hide/move/survive in almost any environment (de la Billiere 1992: 235–49). Most of their work does not involve fighting but rather acting as eyes and ears on the ground to guide other forces; though if necessary, they can storm buildings, capture or kill enemies and clear vital spaces, all with paralysing violence. Given their reputation, SF personnel spend time training and mentoring other elite forces in the world and small detachments can sometimes, surprisingly, turn up at critical moments in conflicts almost anywhere. SF are not only operational in conflicts, however. In their intelligence role they can be used to gauge the trend of events in a tense region, do some covert reconnaissance for likely future operations, or simply establish local contacts that may be useful.

They naturally feature heavily in those conflicts involving British ground forces because of the general conditions that now apply. All modern conflicts, whether the no-war-no-peace grey zones, or even a traditional battle between the forces of established states, tend to be characterised by great ambiguity among the protagonists – between legitimate troops and militias, fighting amateurs and pure civilians – as well as a dynamic battle space where air and maritime forces may be trying to link seamlessly with ground forces (Smith 2006: 267–305). In all cases, the quiet work of SF troops in the most sensitive spots can be critical to success, acting as intelligence, reconnaissance, forward air controllers, saboteurs, etc. SF will not win battles on their own, but for Britain they add real potency to operations and help make the most of its limited total force.

The actual numbers, weapons and force structure of Britain's SF is classified information. Certainly, SAS/SBS combined regular numbers are only assumed to be in the upper hundreds, equivalent roughly to a battalion (the US has around

70,000).[2] Many of the *Hercules* transports, *Chinook*, *Dauphin* and other helicopters and various light vehicles are specially fitted out for SF work and kept ready for use. The SF are believed to choose whatever weapons they need.

Unsurprisingly, Britain's SF have been at full stretch since 2001 with the growth of international terror, war and instability across the Middle East and South Asia. The British government does not comment on the existence, operations, the costs or the losses, of SF. Very few individual SF troops have broken the code of silence either. There are good political and operational reasons for this, but the use of British SF troops has become more widespread and Parliament and non-governmental organisations have expressed growing concern over ever more operations that are beyond democratic oversight or accountability (Rogers 2016a; Hansard 2017).

Notes

1   In 2015 this number was required to fall to 41,000 by 2020, but little progress had been made towards this target by 2018.

2   Though the US defines 'Special Forces' far more widely and integrates them into a separate US Special Operations Command (USSOCOM).

4

Wars: military operations

THE Cold War ended dramatically on 26 December 1991 when the collapsed Soviet Union dissolved itself. Ironically, in late 1991 British forces were just returning from the war to help liberate Kuwait from Iraqi occupation, where they had fought with their airpower and heavy metal very much in Cold War style. It was as if anti-Soviet battle routines had been transposed out of NATO and tested by the allies in the open territory around Basra. Britain created a full division for the operation and controlled its own piece of battle space in a conventional war (Freedman and Karsh 1993). In March 2003, in more controversial circumstances, Britain did something similar; creating a fighting division which took control of the southern sector of Iraq in what was again an essentially traditional battle (Smith 1992).

These were by far the biggest military operations British forces had undertaken since the Suez war in 1956 or the Korean war of 1950–53. They featured conventional military forces operating in open, three-dimensional battle spaces, not highly populated between the major cities that were the focus of control, and for clear objectives to defeat Saddam Hussein's forces. In the manner of the 1982 Falklands War, opposing forces competed in recognisable battles to determine the political outcome at the end of the fighting.

Nevertheless, these operations ran against the military trends of the age and that stunning victory in the '100 hours war' to liberate Kuwait in 1991 set in train a quarter century of near continuous British military operations in foreign places. The forces have seldom been so busy in peacetime. As John Gaddis observed, the world witnessed general peace during the years after 1945 when it was geared up for war; followed by frequent wars when the world expected conditions of peace following the collapse of the Soviet Union (Gaddis 2005: 261–3). British defence policy has felt the full force of this historical paradox.

Contemporary operational thinking is obviously shaped around the way current challenges are interpreted, as discussed in Chapter 5. But it is also shaped around a historical legacy of past operations – the motivations for sending forces into combat, or at least in harm's way – the costs that have been incurred and also some consensus on the record of success.

The motivations of military operations

The political motivations behind military operations are seldom straightforward and are subject to change as operations progress. They become matters of fierce debate, as they did even during the two world wars, where national survival seemed to be at stake. Finding political consistency between one operation and another can seem a fruitless pursuit. Nevertheless, it is possible to discern a political orientation, if not highly consistent objectives, in the busy operational record of British forces in recent years. To put it starkly, British policy moved from preparing and fighting defensive wars to being sent abroad on expeditionary operations with increasingly offensive political intentions.

During the Cold War, British defence policy was built on a strategy of fighting conventional war with air and sea power, armour and big ground formations. The military was scaled and trained for a massive conflict in Europe. The fact that it had other commitments in Brunei, Hong Kong, Oman or the Falklands, or took on postcolonial policing operations, in Malaya, Kenya, Cyprus or Aden, not to mention the longest engagement in recent British history – thirty-eight years of *Operation Banner* in Northern Ireland – were sideshows to the main effort. They were all undertaken defensively to try to preserve a status quo, or else ease an inevitable transition with minimal disruption to the status quo. This essentially defensive thinking continued in military operations for a while after the Cold War (Codner, in Johnson 2014: 13–48). The 1991 war against Iraq, as in the earlier Falklands War, was to liberate a territory that had been conquered by military aggression. In 1992, the early effort to support the UN in Bosnia was to perform humanitarian roles and thereby help preserve a status quo that was threatened by the collapse of Yugoslavia (Kaldor 1999: 57–63). So too, in Sierra Leone in 2000 where warlords had deposed the legitimate government (Dorman 2009). In the 2001 Macedonia operation – a startling example of extremely cheap and completely effective conflict prevention – the country was preserved against contagious fragmentation from its neighbours (Laity 2008; Dannatt 2016: 258–60).

With the (relative) successes of these essentially defensive operations of the 1990s, however, at a time when Russia and other powers could do little to oppose western operations, political expectations in some western capitals became unrealistic. From the opening years of this century many leaders began to assume that a determined application of military force was capable of delivering complex political outcomes. This was despite the fact that, aside from the two wars against Saddam Hussein in 1991 and 2003, all other operations in the three decades since the end of the Cold War took place in quite new circumstances. As characterised by Rupert Smith, these new operations could hardly have been more different. They were, he says, subject to shifting political objectives, conducted 'amongst the people', they created timeless commitments, required improvised weapons and organisation, were fought against non-state organisations, and were greatly constrained by the notion that the force 'must be preserved'. Not least, he points out, there was little appetite for tolerating military casualties (Smith 2006: 267–305).

Notwithstanding the major changes that Smith noted, there was a mood in the US (which pre-dated the 2001 al Qaeda attacks on New York and Washington) and shared in Britain by Tony Blair's government, that has been widely characterised as western hubris over the emerging world order (Codner, in Johnson 2014: 42–7). Britain's experience of colonial operations, it was assumed, would stand it in good stead in the more difficult operations that Smith had described. These difficult 'grey zone' expeditionary conflicts, often defined as 'peace support operations' steadily became more 'offensive' in their intentions and justifications. They aimed to provoke change and shape a new status quo, partly in the belief that core western values were under attack (see Chalmers, in Johnson 2014: 198–200). By 1994 in Bosnia, for instance, it was clear that Yugoslavia could not be rescued, and the US, Britain and France used their military muscle to drive the warring parties to negotiations and effectively impose a new pattern of multiple states on the western Balkans. In Kosovo, they chose to break Serbia up rather than let the government in Belgrade continue to persecute its Albanian minority in that province (Robertson 1999: 7–9). In Afghanistan, they chased out the government that had hosted the al Qaeda terrorists responsible for the 9/11 atrocity, and then tried to transform Afghan society into a modern and democratic economy. A questionable campaign to rid the world of Saddam Hussein's bombastic challenges to international law in 2003 was also an audacious attempt to reshape the whole Levant around a new, democratic Iraq that would be nurtured after a quick and decisive offensive campaign (Frum 2003: 226–31; Freedman 2008: 376, 423–5). In 2011 the immediate impetus to prevent the Gaddafi regime massacring civilians in Libya rapidly turned into a campaign of regime change itself which then destabilised not only Libya but much of the Sahel region to the south. And in the campaign to destroy the terrorist menace of Islamic State in Iraq and Syria, the allies entangled themselves with Kurdish forces on the ground, who were also in the process of trying to create a new Kurdish state across the Levant (Shareef 2017).

These conflicts have been called genuine 'wars of choice', in that they could have been ignored in terms of the essential national security of Britain (Freedman 2010). They all had an indirect bearing on British security, such as maintaining close political ties with the United States, or reinforcing Britain's status as one of the five permanent members of the United Nations Security Council. Some might be justified as combating terrorism as far away from Britain's shores as possible, or maintaining credibility in the eyes of allies. But none of these operations *had* to be fought militarily to keep Britain's homeland or its trading and manufacturing freedoms safe. There were other means of pursuing those ends, and Britain could still balance the possible political costs of not being militarily proactive, against the risks of engagement. Most of Britain's European partners, for example, choose to be far less militarily committed. It was therefore Britain's choice – an instinctive and consistent orientation – to follow the US military lead in nine of the twelve operations it conducted between 1991 and 2018 and to be the second biggest force contributor in all of them (Clarke, in Johnson 2014: 237–65).

Of course, leaders such as Tony Blair or David Cameron argue that they had no intention of going on a political offensive; they were often reacting to events as best they could (Blair 2007; Clarke 2007: 600; Inboden 2010; Cameron 2015). Like US presidents, they were confronted by unique problems in the 9/11 attacks, and all responsible European leaders would have preferred the Balkans and the Middle East not to have erupted in even more factionalism. But political motivations are frequently conflicted and often simply contradictory. Under day-to-day pressures leaders are subject to the momentum of events; the fashionable commentaries, the political mood of an age, and their accumulated decisions often produce results they never consciously intend.

Short-term perspectives also reinforce leaders' instincts. If this offensive orientation appears to have been strategically at odds with what had gone before, it nevertheless had an aura of consistency around it at the time. There was ideological consistency in wanting to protect, and then promote, liberal capitalist democracy when it was coming under pressure a decade after it had seemed triumphant in 1991. This was completely in tune with US thinking which added a strong flavour of British national interest. Tony Blair's Chicago speech in 1999, in which he defined a concept of 'liberal interventionism', was an eloquent expression of many converging strands of old and new thought (Sloboda and Abbott 2004). It also chimed in with emerging US military doctrine that aimed to conduct operations with 'economy of force' and British instincts to achieve its military purposes through greater 'training and support' for friendly forces in operational zones. There was little recognition at the time of how unusually favourable the international constellation of forces had been for the western powers during the 1990s, which was not the long-term norm; and too much faith was placed in 'muscular peacekeeping', as if the hard-won lessons of small operations in the Balkans could easily be transposed to much bigger operations, in different cultural environments, in Afghanistan and Iraq (Strachan, in Bailey et al. 2013: 329).

Post-2014 retrenchment

In 2009 the British operation in Iraq ended, and by December 2014 the withdrawal from Afghanistan was complete. By then both the political and public mood had changed. Confidence in the ability of military operations to produce politically complex outcomes had diminished, alongside a decline in the hitherto strong confidence even in the forces' own ability to prevail militarily. In truth, the mood pendulum had swung too far by 2015, and politicians oversimplified public reticence to military operations (Rogers and Eyal, in Johnson 2014: 187–9). The British military certainly needed no reminders that, by themselves, they were not in the business of manufacturing political outcomes. British chiefs knew only too well that the military can only create the conditions for a political outcome in expeditionary operations – to beat or frustrate an enemy, to buy time, to create physical stalemates so that politicians, civil society or the international community can get to work hammering out something else. All too often, however, the space the military created was left unoccupied by indigenous political leaders, and almost everyone else. In both Iraq and Afghanistan, the national political elites who were empowered by western military intervention proved incapable of forming governments that were sufficiently competent or even legitimate. 'Civil society' in both countries, such as it was, took culturally different forms that did not work in coherent directions; and the 'international community' – the external peace talks, the donor conferences, the aid programmes and the NGO community – as in most post-conflict societies, eventually became part of the problem. Iraq and Afghanistan rapidly fell into a psychology of dependence on the intervening powers. And that meant heavy dependence on the military who were anxious to hand off their responsibilities to local or international civilian organisations, but were unable to do so without creating more instability or feeding rampant corruption. The British military certainly cannot escape all blame for the various failures in Iraq and Afghanistan, but the lack of effective planning for the post-conflict phases in both has appalled and baffled investigators and analysts alike, from the Chilcot Report on Iraq to the worm's-eye view of soldiers in Afghanistan (Simpson 2012; Clarke 2016). Most of this must lie at the door of western (and local) political leaders who were less realistic than their generals over what the military were capable of achieving.

The 2011 Libyan air operation to support local anti-Gaddafi forces on the ground was successful, though not quickly or decisively, but more or less in the way military chiefs had planned. But the irregular Libyan forces that deposed Gaddafi were then anxious to keep western post-conflict involvement in the country to a minimum. Some showed outright hostility. A unified national government was impossible and within months Britain, France, the US and other NATO partners watched helplessly as the country fell into violent civil war and regional destabilisation, providing a haven for more terrorists, and all with access to the massive stockpiles of weapons that Gaddafi had buried throughout Libya (Foreign and Commonwealth Office 2013). In this case it was a post-conflict mess largely of Libyan leaders' own making.

It is not surprising that the Conservative governments of 2015 and 2017 inherited a mood of retrenchment about military operations. Prime Minister David Cameron declared that henceforth only direct national interests would trigger military interventions. Nevertheless, in 2013 the Cameron government failed to get a parliamentary majority to follow the US in punishing Syria's President Assad after he had used chemical weapons against his own people. It was a big moment, regardless of a similar controversy within the US about the issue. In September 2014 the government partially followed the US in launching *Operation Shader* to attack Islamic State in its Iraqi territory, and in December 2015 embraced full participation by extending the air battle zone to Syria. Though these operations undoubtedly achieved their military purpose by the end of 2017, there remained a widespread belief that the same could not be said of their political purposes.

By 2018, for the first time since 1991, Britain was not involved in major combat or peace support operations anywhere else in the world. It provided a historical moment of reflection on the future of the forces. It also took place at a time when Britain's immediate neighbourhood in Europe, the Mediterranean and the Middle East, as well as its functional security for trading, commerce and manufacturing looked far less benign than in the previous decade. This will be discussed further in Chapters 5 and 6.

The costs and success of military operations

Britain undertook twelve significant military campaigns between 1991 and 2018, not counting minor military assistance to allies in operations in East Timor and Mali, or to international organisations in Somalia, South Sudan and the Democratic Republic of Congo.

The twelve operations are represented in Figure 4.1. They ranged from full-on wars in the Middle East to small-scale conflict prevention and, in one way or another, drew on all three services for most of them. More than 758,000 regulars served in the British armed forces from 1991 to 2014 and 235,000 of them were engaged in these major campaigns (Diehle and Greenberg 2016). The Army, however, was the most heavily engaged by the very nature of these particular operations, with the RAF often close to full stretch in protecting, supplying and running the ISTAR for them. The Sierra Leone operation was a genuinely joint endeavour where a small task force composed of all three services quickly achieved its military objectives at very small cost. The operations against Islamic State were overwhelmingly based on RAF resources, though a battalion-sized Army training mission in Iraq was involved and a considerable element of SF were believed also to be active on the ground. The Royal Navy was heavily involved in both Iraq wars and also supplied significant personnel for ground duties, apart from the marine commandos, to operations in Bosnia and then Afghanistan.

As Figure 4.1 indicates, the military success of these operations is generally regarded as high. Only the first Afghanistan operation can be regarded as minimally successful, where British involvement made little strategic difference to the US push to destroy al Qaeda and capture or kill its leaders. The second phase of the operation in 2006 was undertaken largely because the first one was heading for evident failure. Six of the twelve cases, however, can be regarded as totally or mainly successful in military terms; five as partially successful.

In political terms the judgement is not so favourable. Three cases can be regarded as totally successful in that they created exactly the political conditions that were intended – to liberate Kuwait, rescue Sierra Leone's government and prevent a war in Macedonia. But aid to the UNPROFOR operation in Bosnia was hardly successful. It neither delivered enough aid nor stabilised the situation. In the end, US leadership within NATO took over in a different type of operation that can be judged much more successful. The long Iraq operation, successful at first, also has to be judged a strategic failure in that after 2009 very little of what the allies left in place proved to be robust and the great winner from the whole enterprise was Iran – the natural adversary to western influence across the region. And though the second Afghan operation was designed to rescue the first, its

Operation	Direct costs: £bn[1]	Military assessment	Political assessment[2]
1991 Iraq – liberation of Kuwait	0.68	Totally successful	Totally successful
1991–2003 Iraq – no-fly zones over parts of Iraq	0.36	Mainly successful	Partially successful
1992–95 Bosnia – UNPROFOR operations to deliver aid	0.28	Partially successful	Minimally successful
1995–2002 Bosnia – IFOR/SFOR stabilisation operations	1.45	Totally successful	Partially successful
1999–2003 Kosovo – air war against Serbia to secure Kosovo	1.25	Partially successful	Largely successful
2000 Sierra Leone – anti-warlord intervention	0.08	Totally successful	Totally successful
2001 Macedonia – peacekeeping NATO operation	0.01[3]	Totally successful	Totally successful
2001–06 Afghanistan – supporting US forces & stabilisation	1.06	Minimally successful	Largely unsuccessful
2003–09 Iraq – invasion and stabilisation operations	9.56	Partially successful	Unsuccessful
2006–14 Afghanistan – assertive stabilisation in Helmand	23.19[4]	Partially successful	Minimally successful
2011 Libya – air war to help anti-Gaddafi rebels	0.24	Partially successful	Unsuccessful

	Totally successful	Partially successful
2014–2018 Iraq / Syria – air operations against 'Islamic State'		0.29[5]
Total		38.45[6]

Figure 4.1 British military combat operations since the Cold War

1 Figures from Malcolm Chalmers, in Johnson (2014: 268), except where specified. Costs are standardised as far as possible in 2012/13 prices.

2 Both military and political categories are personal assessments by the author and based mainly on previous research reported in Johnson (2014: 237–65).

3 In the event, this was not a combat operation, though the deployment took place on the basis that it could be, if its deterrent mission had failed. It cost £1 million in cash terms reported in 2003–04; worth £1.2m in 2012/13 real terms, as analysed by Chalmers, in Johnson (2014: 289).

4 This figure represents declared costs of £19.59 billion up to 2013, before the operation wound down in 2014, as calculated by Chalmers, in Johnson (2014: 268). If the estimated costs for 2012 to 2013 were repeated in 2013–14, this would add some £3.6 billion, giving a final total of £23.19 billion. On the annualised estimated costs, see House of Commons Library (2012: 5).

5 This figure reflects costs reported by the MoD to Parliament in February 2017, covering the period September 2014 to March 2016. It also includes figures of some £23m per annum from the Deployed Military Activity Pool – most, but not all, of which covers training for Kurdish and Iraqi forces (House of Commons Library (2017b)). The true total cost up to 2018 when the operation wound down might therefore be estimated around £320 to £325 million in 2012/13 prices.

6 This total excludes a figure of .24 billion (£245.4 million) for military assistance to other operations in Mali, the Democratic Republic of the Congo and for over-flights and support to other security initiatives in the Gulf.

political outcome can only be regarded as minimally successful in strategic terms, leaving behind an Afghanistan that barely coped with renewed civil war and again became a haven for Islamist terror groups. Finally, the western world may have been glad to see the end of the Gaddafi regime in Libya, but none of its immediate strategic objectives were well served by the operation. The whole scorecard indicates that a generally favourable picture of British military performance did not translate naturally into political effectiveness during these years, particularly in view of the size and importance of the second Iraq and the second Afghan operations.

The material costs of these operations, excluding spending on veterans' care, can be calculated as somewhere between £38.4 billion and approximately £47 billion, at 2012/13 prices. The lower figure is based on official announcements and some extrapolation; the higher figure on other analyses that have tried to factor in the material costs of death and injury in long-term payments, care and support, though not all of these would be borne by government (Ledwidge 2013). The total official figure equates to around 5% to 6% of the average defence budgets across the period. This reflects the fact that, in material terms, operations are not as expensive as is often assumed. They involve the *net additional* cost of sending on operations forces that have to be paid for in any case. The Treasury covers these, though there is normally a tough negotiation between the MoD and the Treasury over what should be regarded as 'net additional'. Then, too, there are one-off issues. Operating as a UN peacekeeper attracts payments per head from the UN. Unusually, the costs of the 1991 war against Iraq were almost all recouped from burden-sharing agreements with Saudi Arabia, Kuwait, Germany and Japan.

If the material costs seem generally low, other factors should also be recognised. Such calculations take no account of opportunity costs – what else the forces might have been doing, or what reorganisations and economies did not take place because of the relentless drumbeat of operations. At its peak, the 2006–14 Afghanistan operation absorbed the efforts of almost 50% of Britain's available ground forces. Or again, care for veterans, historically low in Britain, might demand far more – around 66,000 ex-service personnel might need long-term health support (Diehle and Greenberg 2016). Most eye-catching, however, is the fact that the second Iraq and the second Afghanistan operations together amounted to £32.75 billion, just over 85% of the total for all twelve operations.

The immediate human costs can also be estimated, though longer-term consequences are always uncertain. Figure 4.2 offers a glimpse of the human losses involved.

The list of military fatalities provides interesting comparisons with the 371 troops killed in Cyprus since 1955, or the 1,441 in Northern Ireland, or the 2,572 killed between 1948 and 1960 in Malaya and Korea (MoD 2016a).

Constant and *relentless* operations

The armed forces are not always involved in combat. Even after the end of operations in Afghanistan and with the long-term withdrawal from Germany, around 9,000 service personnel and 5,000 MoD civilians are normally located overseas (MoD 2016b). The forces have standing commitments to the fourteen British Overseas Territories and their quarter of a million inhabitants, and they regularly operate in them, particularly in the Falklands, Gibraltar, the two sovereign base areas of Cyprus and Ascension Island. Army and RAF elements are committed for the foreseeable future in a conventional deterrent role in the Baltic States. In 2017 the RAF took the NATO lead in sending *Typhoon* fighters to Romania. All three services maintain facilities in the Gulf – a new naval base in Bahrain, a key air headquarters outside Doha, and a major logistics hub at the Minhad airbase in the United Arab Emirates. The navy regularly contributes to international anti-piracy missions. There are British training facilities in Canada and Belize, longstanding training missions in Kenya and Nigeria, a Gurkha battalion and a training base in Brunei and ad hoc technical and medical assistance has been sent to countries as diverse as Sierra Leone, Somalia and Nepal. Not

| Operation | British military personnel | | Est. civilian in-theatre[1] |
	Dead	Seriously wounded[2]	Deaths
1991 Iraq – liberation of Kuwait	47	811	3,500[3]
1991–2003 Iraq – no-fly zones over parts of Iraq	7	0	None reported
1992–present[4] Bosnia/UNPROFOR/IFOR/SFOR/Kosovo/Macedonia	72	79	108,000[5]
2000 Sierra Leone – anti-warlord intervention	5	0	50–200[6]
2001–present[7] Afghanistan/ 01–06/06–14	456	616[8]	27,000[9]
2003–2011 Iraq	178	222[10]	120,000[11]
2011 Libya – air war to help anti-Gaddafi rebels	1	0	4,800[12]
2014–18 Iraq / Syria – air operations against 'Islamic State'	2[13]	0	17,000–25,000[14]

Figure 4.2   The human cost of combat operations since the Cold War

1 In-theatre civilian deaths are very difficult to establish precisely, and figures are often fiercely contested. These figures represent estimated violent deaths from all sources during the periods of British military involvement, including from forces Britain was fighting.

2 Those treated in, or evacuated from, the battle zone is frequently a high number, but official figures normally distinguish the 'very seriously injured'/'seriously injured' as a meaningful metric for comparison.

3 Project on Defense Alternatives, 20 October 2003, rounding down an accepted figure of 3,664.

4 These operations are conflated in official MoD figures. No official deconstructed figures are published outside

regimental records. These figures compiled from House of Commons Debates, National Archives, and Journal of the Royal Army Medical Corps, 2004.

5 The International Criminal Tribunal on Yugoslavia Demographic Unit records over 34,000 civilian deaths plus almost 70,000 deaths among Bosnian, Serb and Croat militias. Human Rights Watch and Post-War Suffering offer a confirmed (but not total) number of 3,150 civilian deaths in the Kosovo crisis.

6 Reported deaths in 2000 only, following a civil war that began in 1991. Conciliation Resources Accord on Sierra Leone, 2015/Tufts University.

7 These operations are conflated in official MoD figures. No official deconstructed figures are published outside regimental records. Time series data, however, shows 10 deaths from 2001–2005, 444 from 2006–14 and 2 in 2015. MoD statistics, 2015.

8 Ministry of Defence, UK Forces: Operations in Afghanistan, 19 January 2015.

9 Figures from United Nations Assistance Mission to Afghanistan, UNAMA Annual Report 2015, also 2010. Figures reflect civilian deaths since 2006. Prior to that, relatively small numbers were involved in operations 2001–05.

10 Ministry of Defence, Operations in Iraq: British Casualties, 3 December 2012.

11 Estimated by Iraq Body Count, Database, 2018. Other sources have higher estimates, but IBC is the best regarded source.

12 Estimated that 2,000 caused by government forces, 1,700 by rebel forces and 1,100 by airstrikes. Drawn from collated Wikipedia reports.

13 Deaths reported on ground training operations in Iraq, The Independent, 4 January 2017; Daily Telegraph, 2 February 2018.

14 Airwars, 20 January 2018. Of this total Airwars estimate civilian fatalities from US-led coalition action to be between 11,071 and 16,809. Some 732 deaths are acknowledged by the coalition. The MoD contend that they have no confirmed evidence of civilian deaths resulting from British actions, but critics point out that they do not look for any.

least, after Afghanistan the armed forces committed themselves to extensive 'defence engagement' around the world, to develop partnerships and increase their own cultural understanding of changing regional dynamics.

One other ongoing military operation is completely anomalous to all this. *Operation Relentless* is the latest iteration of a mission that began in 1968; to maintain nuclear deterrent submarines on patrol constantly and without any breaks to ensure that one boat is always available and ready to fire its nuclear missiles if necessary. The crews of what the Royal Navy refers to as the 'bombers' maintain that they are always at war, cruising beneath the Atlantic on a permanent war footing. Theirs is a deterrent war and it goes on silently and permanently, regardless of what happens elsewhere in British defence policy. They maintain continuous at-sea deterrence (CASD). If they ever fired their missiles in anger, they would have lost their war; the deterrent would have failed.

Britain originally decided to become an independent nuclear power in 1946 and in the years since then every argument about that status has been rehearsed many times over; sometimes as part of a general election campaign, as in 1983; more usually in the midst of multi-term governments, as happened in the late 1950s, the mid 1960s and throughout the 1980s (Gill 2014). Over this time the broad trends of British public opinion about the country's nuclear forces have not changed very much, though they spike around particular issues in some years. Depending on how the questions are asked, however, the long-term trends of opinion are that up to 60% of the public believe Britain should operate nuclear weapons for as long as other states in the world possess them; about 25% of the public oppose nuclear weapons regardless, and 15% or more are inclined to lean either way depending on circumstances (Jones and Reece 1990; Ritchie and Ingram 2013; YouGov UK 2013).

Arguments between and among these sections of opinion have ranged from the philosophical to the staunchly practical. There are powerful arguments as well as many illogical ones on all sides of the debate. Many anti-nuclear campaigners argue that nuclear weapons are morally wrong by their very nature – they are weapons of mass and indiscriminate destruction and should be banned by the United Nations in the same way that chemical and biological weapons, or anti-personnel landmines, are banned. Others argue that history no longer offers such moral high ground but rather a mid-level patch of relative virtue that regards nuclear weapons as posing a powerful ethical dilemma (Quinlan 2009). So long as they continue to exist and proliferate across the world, it is better for Britain to be one of the nuclear powers and put itself in a position to influence multilateral disarmament. In this view, being a responsible nuclear power, being committed to multilateral disarmament and to maintaining a minimum nuclear deterrent, sufficient only for last-ditch national defence, is the best moral compromise in a dangerous world. Sceptics see this position as a post hoc justification for a slimmed-down nuclear force that has never been based on more than political instinct, still less on some precise calculation of what 'minimum deterrence' requires (Ritchie 2012: 13).

Deterrence, of course, is entirely a matter of belief. If two or more states believe they feel the power of deterrence – singly or mutually – then it certainly exists. If they do not, then it does not. Strategic arguments about deterrence are therefore very difficult to verify. Some idea of how nuclear deterrence might possibly have worked in the past may be gleaned from the history of leaders' reactions and memories from previous policies and events. But it is problematical to project any conclusions into the future where the strategic context will assuredly be different. A condition of 'deterrence' might reasonably be assumed, but it can never be taken for granted.

An equal amount of heat has also been generated by disputes on more practical matters. Some have argued that Britain does not operate a genuinely independent deterrent. It is true that the British nuclear force is deeply linked to US technology and ongoing support. But it is also true that it is operated independently and will always be able to fire its missiles at its own volition. Others have argued that it costs too much. Its absolute cost is certainly high, but it has always constituted a

manageable proportion of total defence budgets over its operational lifetime. The new deterrent force from the 2030s to the
2060s is not expected to be any different. On the other hand, it is
suggested that cyberattack or the use of undersea robots could
render the British force vulnerable or impotent within this long
lifetime; claims that are so far only speculative (Ingram 2015).
Supporters of the nuclear deterrent also point to the technology
and skilled jobs that it supports; or the international prestige it
brings to Britain's image in the world. Opponents regard the
economic benefits as irrelevant in the context of mass life and
death calculations involved in nuclear strategy, and are frankly
contemptuous that nuclear power brings Britain anything other
than derision when its overall status in the world is so reduced.

The most prescient contemporary argument about Britain's
independent nuclear deterrent can be expressed in a telling comment made by one of the great moral and political theorists of
Britain's nuclear forces, Sir Michael Quinlan, after he retired in
1992 as head of the MoD. He said that if Britain were not already
a nuclear power, it would be hard to imagine it now deciding to
become one. But – and here is the moral mid-ground – given
that it *is* a nuclear power, and can afford to remain one, it made
sense to preserve its nuclear force as an insurance policy and as
leverage into global diplomacy and arms control negotiations
(Quinlan 2011: 220; Stocker 2007). Critics wonder whether strategic reasoning should really be so casual; nuclear weapons as
afterthoughts (Stephens 2006).

This wide span of argument is not replicated in the same
way in the US and hardly evident in France – Europe's only other
nuclear power – nor within nuclear-armed Israel. There is no dis-
cernible public discussion at all in other nuclear weapons states;
Russia, China, India, Pakistan and North Korea. Britain's nuclear
debates, however, have run through all sectors of the political
establishment, not excluding the military chiefs. For them, it has
not centred on moral questions so much as whether an independent nuclear deterrent is an appropriate way to guarantee
British security and the opportunity costs of spending money on
it. Successive governments, however, have been robust in their

justification for it. In 2006 the government resolved to renew the present force so that a new generation of submarines and weapons would take the deterrent well into the 2060s, and in 2007 Parliament confirmed that intention.

The present *Vanguard* force of four submarines will be replaced by four new *Dreadnought*-class boats that will begin coming into service 'from the 2030s onwards' (MoD 2016c) – later than the MoD had planned, where the old force is at the limit of its realistic life extension. The boats are built by BAE Systems in Britain; they will be nuclear powered by Rolls-Royce PWR 3 reactors. They will still carry Trident D-5 missiles which are produced in the US and, in effect, are leased by Britain, which receives and exchanges missiles as British boats go in and out of King's Bay, Georgia where Trident missiles are stored. The warheads themselves are produced in Britain to a design said to be a copy of US designs. A *Dreadnought* boat will carry eight Trident missiles, each capable of delivering up to five separate warheads, forty in total. Only one, or possibly two, boats are kept nuclear armed and with *Dreadnought* Britain's nuclear inventory will be reduced from some 160 warheads to around 120 (Hennessy and Jinks 2015: 660–8).

The acquisition cost of the new deterrent programme is put at £31 billion, though the government has allocated a uniquely high figure of £10 billion as 'contingency', which suggests that the programme will eventually cost close to £41 billion (MoD 2016c). Running costs thereafter are expected to be in the region of £2.5 to £3 billion a year for its thirty-year lifespan (House of Commons Library 2015b: 21). These costs will represent around 5% to 6% of the defence budget (on present trends) over the course of its full life; though the financial squeeze is tight in the early 2020s during the peak spending period.

Though they operate alone, the Trident boats require some support. Hunter-killer submarines protect them in shallower waters near Britain, and as they set out or return to base from their three-month patrols, the underwater channels they use are swept, protected and closely monitored by air, sea, undersea and shore-based systems. Though they disappear very effectively while on patrol, the bombers constantly exercise and test. Their busyness is all to anticipate the appalling moment when a captain might be called on to fire; or else to open the prime minister's sealed letter with standing instructions on what to do (Hennessy and Jinks 2015: 674–5). And if a prime minister ever gave the order to fire, the bomber would do so 55 minutes later.

5

Strategies: turning geopolitical wheels

DEFENCE policy analysts learn to be cautious. Any country's defence policy, at any time in its history, seems to be at a 'crossroads' when viewed by its contemporaries. All choices look difficult before they are made, and Britain obviously faces some challenging questions about its security and defence policy for the 2020s. Its operational history, as described in Chapter 4, has gone from Cold War military stalemate, to active expeditionary warfare – first to preserve a status quo, then increasingly to change it – and thence into a period of retrenchment where it struggled to afford its ambitious equipment programme. The context is always shifting. Defence is the most officially reviewed policy area in Whitehall. The 2018 defence review was the fourteenth formal review since 1945, not counting all the informal 'refresh' exercises (Hennessy 2013: 26–9). While defence does not rank as the most troubled ministry in Whitehall, it is, as described in previous chapters, an existentially soul-searching, cash-strapped organisation.

After 2015, defence faced a genuine moment of reflection about Britain's objectives – what it is trying to defend in a globalised world – and its expectations, as the twenty-first century confounds so many political assumptions that were made in the twentieth. There is now more than enough evidence to suggest that the questions British defence policy will have to answer in the coming decade are more than averagely tough. They *are* strategically fundamental as the geopolitical wheels of world politics remorselessly turn.

The problem of strategy

There are endless debates in defence studies about strategy (see Melvin 2012). Some contend that attempts to have a strategy are simply misplaced; real life dictates what leaders have to do, and they simply reach for their survival instincts to cope with the pressures of events (Gaskarth 2015). Others misquote the shadowy figure of Sun Tsu in *The Art of War* who only apocryphally said that 'Strategy without tactics is the slowest route to victory. Tactics without strategy is the noise before defeat' (Kaplan 2002: 40–4).

The practical reality for defence planners is not whether there is, or is not, a strategy, but rather at what level of abstraction it exists (Freedman 2013: 237–44). For decades, Britain had a clear national orientation which was never all written down in a single government document, but which acted as a consistent 'grand strategy' for over sixty years; staying close to the United States, opposing Soviet hegemony, transitioning an empire to independence, and playing an active role in the world order Britain had helped to shape while disguising continued economic decline. In defence terms, the ideology of containment and Britain's extensive roles in NATO provided a solid framework that substituted for any agonising over what the country's essential strategy should be. Switches in policy, like the withdrawal from East of Suez, or the attempt (in 1957) to rely more on nuclear forces or (in 1981) less on the Royal Navy, all remained firmly within this national orientation. In fact, British leaders had not needed to think very strategically since the appeasement/rearmament debates of the 1930s. The imperatives of the Empire, the Second World War and then the Cold War were all very powerful.

By the late 1990s, however, those assumptions had been overtaken by events and the same imperatives no longer applied. Not surprisingly, defence then produced a clutch of rather specific strategy documents that went deep into the governmental machinery to create a series of policy blueprints. National security strategy increasingly took on the appearance of business strategy, with its focus on efficiency and management. There is no effective 'blueprint' for the future of national security; world politics is more than a marketplace and the objectives of politics are more multidimensional than anything in the business world. The tendency to regard efficiency strategy as synonymous with national strategy became so persistent that in 2009 the CDS issued a clarion call for the country and its government to match *meaningful* national policy ends with the ways and resources for achieving them. Betting whole defence budgets on predictions of the future is a losing game. But so is refusing to make any major policy assumptions when significant national resources have to be allocated. What the CDS called for was a rediscovery of that discipline of thinking that is strategically literate enough to match ends, ways and means as the country steered itself through the treacherous waters of global politics; sometimes with continuity but also with sharp change as it might seem necessary (Porter 2010). Good strategy, in this view, is not a document, still less a blueprint. Nor is it a single policy, to be maintained regardless. It is, instead, an explicit awareness of clear national priorities and a way of thinking throughout the system (not just among political leaders and chiefs) about the realistic trade-offs to be made in adopting and maintaining strategic coherence as the country reacts to events. As President Eisenhower observed in 1957 reflecting on his military experience, 'Plans are worthless, but planning is everything'.

In the view of most analysts, this 2009 challenge has not been adequately met. The first, true post-Cold War defence review was that of the incoming Labour government in 1998. This review made explicit a series of assumptions about the UK's role in the world after the Cold War and built a future force structure around them. In essence, those assumptions were, first, that Britain's global interests drive a series of global commitments on behalf of world order; as it was expressed, 'we must be prepared to go to the crisis rather than have the crisis come to us' (MoD 1998: 2). Second, therefore, Britain must maintain the capacity to be proactive in defence and security, which in 1998 meant more of the expeditionary operations that had already become a feature of British policy. Third, defence and security must mobilise all instruments of national power to achieve its various aims; military, diplomatic, economic, including foreign aid and sometimes also with home affairs. Fourth, Britain would work even harder on its alliances and partnerships, since the vast majority of what it would do in defence and security could only realistically be achieved through coalitions. The Unites States was critical and Britain's international partnering networks, therefore, all operated outwards from the Atlantic Alliance. Britain's role as a 'bridge' between the US and its main European allies in NATO was both the essence of its security in Europe and the mechanism that also made Britain an attractive military partner outside the NATO context.

On these assumptions the Royal Navy began to structure itself around the creation of a powerful carrier battle group, the Army around lighter mobile brigades from which land battle groups could be quickly deployed, and the RAF around new expeditionary air wings that could operate from other centres in southern Europe or the Middle East. In 1998, in other words, the assumptions that were then spelled out really did drive the future force structure in the armed services (though to differing degrees in each). For a time, an attractive slogan gained currency that the forces were structured to 'go first, go fast, go home', until that was belied by the realities of operations that required them to be sustained for a long time after any combat (Dannatt 2016: 252). Nevertheless, the 1998 review was an exercise in strategic thinking in that it tried to reconcile ends, ways and means. It was not entirely successful since the financial element of the 'means' was unrealistic and based on the most favourable economic projections. But it set a direction on the basis of assumptions about the nature of the world after the Cold War.

There have been three major defence reviews since the 1998 exercise, in 2010, 2015 and 2018 and they have all been concerned not with the continuing validity of these assumptions, but, rather, whether the force structure and the money available for it, were adequate to deliver on them. This is not surprising because the answer is very difficult to discover. If the task of a defence review was simply to match static force structures to stated objectives, it would be relatively easy. But the process is full of political imponderables such as the *scale* and the *speed* at which it might be necessary to operate, whether operations might be *concurrent* or sequential, what levels of *readiness* are acceptable, which regular *allies* might be involved, or the *geographical demands* of likely operational areas, to mention only the most obvious.

Yet in the years after 1998 the geopolitical wheels continued their remorseless turning, sometimes very quickly. In 2001 the 9/11 attacks on the US took place, and, in Tony Blair's words, 'the world had changed' (Blair 2010: 342). Three months after the 2010 review the Arab Uprising changed the geopolitics of the Middle East more profoundly than anything since the First World War. The global economic crisis was biting into the politics of all western countries, and Russia's annexation of Crimea in 2014 amid the Ukraine crisis, marked the first time since the 1930s that European borders had been changed through external aggression. One year after the 2015 review, Britain voted to leave the EU, and to the even greater astonishment of the political world, Donald Trump rode a wave of populism in the United States to become president. And notwithstanding Russia's explicitly declared territorial revisionism,[1] persistent European refugee crises and deepening strategic failure in both Iraq and Afghanistan, the two-part security review of 2018 still maintained that all such developments were within the operating assumptions of Britain's defence strategy. Only their speed and severity was unexpected. While commentators wondered what, in that case, would ever fall outside the working assumptions, official attention remained focused on the adequacy of the force structure to back them up.

It again comes down to the level at which defence strategy is pitched (Heuser 2010: 27–8). There is general agreement that bringing more business efficiency into defence policy, as the much-needed Levene reforms did after 2010, should not be confused with national strategy (Levene 2011: 9). But there is continued disquiet that strategic assumptions have continued to be so generic in the face of myriad new challenges as to be unhelpful in making meaningful resource choices – matching ends to ways and means. The first part of the 2018 review reaffirmed that Britain's interests lay in protecting and promoting the 'rules-based international order', that defence should contribute to a 'prosperity agenda' and that Britain's forces should ultimately be capable of sustaining 'modern deterrence' to protect the country and its interests (HM Government 2018: 7–11). These are intellectually sound enough organising principles that would apply whether the country was facing the world in 1998 or twenty years later. In truth, almost any defence budget or force structure can be made to look appropriate to such generic aspirations. The argument for bringing real defence and security strategy down one level to address more directly the great changes in world politics since 1998 is very strong, even if strategy at this lower level is not publicly acknowledged. Perhaps, it is said, this is how it really works (Edmunds 2014).

Myriad new security challenges

National security challenges always come in multiples rather than single instances. That is to be expected. They exist along a spectrum. The spectrum of security risks for any country can range from internal disorder or disease, crime and terrorism, cyber threats to its infrastructure or threats to its pillars of prosperity, military threats in its region or to its allies, challenges to its essential interests abroad, right up to wars of aggression against it. Governments have to manage the relative risks they pose by assessing both the severity and the likelihood of their occurrence. In 2008 the British government began producing a National Risk Register and a three-tier 'national security risk assessment' that covered the spectrum in exactly this way (Cabinet Office 2008; MoD 2010).

The contemporary security spectrum which the risk matrix addresses appears to be characterised by three inescapable megatrends that have manifested themselves in the decade since 2008: increased global disorder involving a sharp decline in the long-standing rules of international order; much greater complexity and volatility in the workings of global politics; and a return to the prospect of interstate strategic and military confrontation, in addition to all the fragmentation and non-state violence that has been evident since the 1990s (Pentagon 2018). A great deal could be written about each of them, but even in barest outline, such megatrends are transformative in comparison with the global politics of the last thirty years; realities well recognised in western capitals (French White Paper 2013; Defence Concepts and Doctrine Centre [hereafter DCDC] 2014; NIC 2017).

For a country such as Britain this means that the security risk spectrum is wider than ever before, more prone to throwing up greater risks from areas that were previously low risk, and shows some contagion of insecurity from one region and one issue to another. For example, two decades ago, cyber power outside Britain could be seen as a challenge to the culture and economic performance of the country. Now it also has to be classified either as a security threat in itself, in the form of cyberwar; or more likely as part of a related security threat – serious international crime, terrorism or a distraction attack by an enemy taking military action elsewhere (Rid 2013). Two decades ago, terrorism was a limited domestic threat, in that Britain effectively neutralised both Irish republican and loyalist terror, and certainly contained the foreign terror threat that was first manifest in the late 1990s. But since then terrorism has become a completely global phenomenon that has the potential to undermine social cohesion in Britain in significant ways, and there is little the government can do directly to diminish its international mainsprings.

Or again, civil technologies have always been incorporated into military systems where they offer advantages. But rapid breakthroughs even since 2010 in computing, artificial intelligence, robotics and microbiological sciences raise possibilities that highly sophisticated military systems might be neutralised cheaply and decisively. Technology may be throwing up game-changing innovations that are available to smaller military powers and in some cases even to high-end non-governmental groups. As Matthew Symonds (2018: 10) put it, 'While America and its allies have spent much of the past 15 years fighting wars against irregular forces in the Middle East and Afghanistan, its adversaries have been studying vulnerabilities in the western way of warfare and exploiting technologies that have become cheaper and more readily available. They have also benefited from research and development passing from military institutions to the civil and commercial sectors.' Of course, the major military powers address these possibilities by trying to stay ahead themselves in such technologies. But this is a very expensive road down which a mid-level military power like Britain must go. It poses severe trade-offs between traditional weapons and new technologies, and also between different technologies in deciding which are worth some heavy spending to stay on the crest of the innovative wave.

Then there is the problem of contagion across the risk spectrum. During the Cold War most security problems tended to be contagious. Local disputes in Africa or Latin America became global security issues precisely because of the competition between superpowers. That phenomenon seemed to disappear in the 1990s and security issues around the world were treated largely as isolated problems. But globalisation has recreated a different sort of contagion between types and areas of instability. Physical mobility between one crisis zone and another for fighters, weapons, money and information has never been easier. Cities and links between them in land-connected countries turn out to be contagious routes for conflict and political instability (Corera 2018). Clever civil technologies are rapidly adapted by international criminal groups, terrorists and rogue states who can maraud across ever-expanding cyberspace that has no temporal or spatial limits. And the knowledge of what is happening in one place is very difficult to keep from seeping into another or from encouraging imitative political behaviour. In the present era, at least, modern technology has dramatically increased the power of 'networks' in relation to the established power of 'governments' (Ferguson 2017: 425). As Henry Kissinger eloquently explained in his study of world order, many traditional security problems persist in new guises, while previously unforeseen problems that are conceptually new stretch our imaginations as we struggle to grasp their impact, let alone prepare for them (Kissinger 2014: 363–5).

In short, the spectrum of political and technological challenges facing Britain, and its western partners, has continued to expand over the last two decades. It is not that the spectrum just shifts focus from one thing to another as events move on. In recent years few lights have gone out on the security risk dashboard; while more continue to flick on, reflecting a range of issues that would not previously have figured as evident 'security risks'.

British strategic policymaking

This array of challenges is daunting, and it is natural that British military and civilian leaders have tried in good faith to address them at the right and most practical levels. 'So what', it might be said, 'if public documents on Britain's strategic objectives are all banal statements of the obvious? As long as real decision-makers have an effective strategy between themselves, surely it hardly matters what they put into the public domain?' That, after all, was how Winston Churchill and General Alan Brooke worked during the Second World War and they operated arguably the most successful strategic partnership in modern British history (Roberts 2008). But that was total war when other priorities could be ignored, and the political environment of the 1940s was so far away from the 2020s that it might as well have been the eighteenth century.

Since 1998 British defence planners have been acutely aware that dealing with the wide spectrum of complex challenges outlined above requires a 'whole of government' approach. After writing it into the 1998 review the Blair government made strenuous efforts to mobilise all relevant ministries towards clear foreign and defence policy objectives (Clarke 2007: 599). It is an entirely sensible and obvious aim. But as successive governments discovered, it is also genuinely difficult to make happen. Different ministries and agencies have their own strong priorities; they have little budget to spare for something that is not their core business and what is presented as a whole-of-government response within Whitehall and enshrined in impressive joint strategy documents too often seemed tokenistic and under-resourced when translated to the sharp end of foreign operations.

This is the answer to the 'so what?' question. It is simply impossible to imagine political and military leaders operating a peacetime strategic design that is pitched at the right level and only shared privately among themselves. Public documents and statements matter, because an ever-changing cast of ministers and a good proportion of the 400,000 civil servants in central government need to understand the objectives if a whole-of-government approach is to be effective. Parliament and related agencies scrutinise policy more closely as never before, and in the networked world that empowers meta-trends of public opinion, the general population has to be content that it more or less understands what security policy is designed to do. Where this is not the case, policy quickly becomes volatile and subject to short-term political tactics. There are good reasons, in other words, to judge British strategic thinking by what successive governments say about it in their key documents.

Notwithstanding all the generalised abstractions of modern strategy statements, it should nevertheless be recognised that successive British governments made some genuine attempts after 1998 to create more coherence from the centre. The COBRA crisis management facility began as an ad hoc arrangement and then developed into a well-orchestrated structure to deal with national emergencies of any sort.[2] Earlier 'post-conflict stabilisation' initiatives abroad were coordinated after 2007 by an upgraded Stabilisation Unit. And a reserve of money was created in two 'conflict prevention pools' in 2001, merged in 2008, and then upgraded to more than £1 billion a year in 2015 in the Conflict Stability and Security Fund. Specific priorities for this were set from the centre (House of Lords 2017: 6). Across Whitehall, in fact, Britain has always been better than most of its partners at internal policy coordination.

Above all, the 2010 government upgraded the cabinet committee charged with coordinating security and defence matters into a full National Security Council (NSC), headed by a national security adviser, with deputies and a small, expert staff. The NSC, chaired by the prime minister, includes all the relevant ministers, the CDS and heads of the intelligence agencies. It is supported by the equivalent officials from around Whitehall who meet separately and shadow its work. The NSC, however, is not at all like its counterpart in Washington where a powerful national security adviser works alongside the president. In a cabinet system, it would be very difficult officially to interpose a non-elected individual (or even an elected one) in between the prime minister and the foreign secretary, chancellor and minister of defence. Nor is the British NSC remotely comparable in size, or its external networks, to its American namesake. The reality is that the British NSC is a good coordinating and liaison body. The national security adviser works closely with the prime minister's own personal advisers on foreign and security policy. They constitute a close team, but they remain, nevertheless, civil servants, not political figures responsible to parliament or the public for Britain's strategic posture. While the NSC worked well in its first decade, the question persisted in Parliament's various oversight committees and around the Westminster bazaars as to whether it really constituted a 'strategic brain' at the apex of government, or merely a better heart to pump the lifeblood of information around the system (Devanny and Harris 2014).

In 2010 the twelfth defence review since 1945 was the first to be directed from the Cabinet Office rather than from the MoD. It also initiated a regular five-yearly review process that would henceforth be directed by the new NSC, inside the Cabinet Office. All aspects of government could be integrated into a coherent approach to the multi-sector security challenges that Britain faced. In 2018, confronted by another hole in its budget and to escape more immediate spending cuts, the MoD successfully separated itself from the National Security Capability Review, and thereby created a two-stage review process. This was the result of an open political struggle between the MoD and the Treasury. Peter Ricketts, a former National Security Adviser, remarked that after efforts 'over the past 10 to 15 years to make all departments that dealt with defence and security issues more joined up ... it's a backward step', but, he said, 'I can imagine the politics behind it' (*Times* 2018).

There is a structural mismatch between the MoD and the rest of Whitehall when it comes to strategic reviews. The MoD has been reviewed so often and so recently that it is good at the process. It has a large staff to go methodically through multiple work streams simultaneously – seventy or more separate work streams are not uncommon during reviews. It embodies industry and military staff who are experienced planners and it always begins detailed work early since its 200,000 employees and the £15 billion it spends annually on defence equipment create a long tail of consequences for any policy changes. The MoD is normally earlier and better prepared than other government departments (or the Cabinet Office) for any defence review. But this does not necessarily help the strategy process. Prior to 1998, defence reviews were, by default, full strategic reviews. Only Downing Street had oversight of them. Even in 1998 the MoD, in effect, had to define for itself what the national strategic objectives were.[3] And in reviews thereafter MoD officials had to pursue their detailed work streams before clear strategic direction was articulated from the centre, or else puzzle over how to fit their ongoing work into the high-level abstractions – in some cases the mere slogans – that were used to describe national security strategy. In an ideal world strategic reviews would involve an iterative process where ends, ways and means were under constant refinement between the MoD, other ministries, the NSC and Downing Street. But at least for the MoD, reviews are such big events, with such long tails of consequences, that it can only handle them in a linear fashion – and only once in a while.

Global strategic realities

The strategic realities for significant, second-rank powers like Britain are ultimately tough and simple. Strategies are built on many intangible things, but they need resources. Strategic change or adaptation normally requires significant shifts of resources to make a meaningful policy impact. Big powers have significant resources but there is little margin of error for second-rank powers when they deploy one-shot forces that are expensive to sustain, or diplomatic and soft power assets that are spread very thinly. Big powers can make strategic mistakes and quickly recover or compensate for them; smaller powers normally suffer the full consequences of their mistakes. Lesser powers naturally become risk-averse and hope to gain strategic leverage from small adjustments and limited action. The problem for powers like Britain is that global geopolitics are again moving towards the domination of the very big players, but with a revised cast of characters. It is accepted that China is now simply 'the biggest player in the history of the world' and strategists worry whether China and the US are predeterminedly 'destined for war' (Coker 2015; Allison 2017: 6). India is resolved to compete with China; Russia is condemned to compete with it, and other players like Indonesia, Iran or Turkey are propelled by their own size towards leadership roles in their respective regions.

The rising power of China was expressed in 2013 by a major strategic switch that Beijing launched to create a unique 'Belt and Road Initiative' across central Asia to Europe and other key destinations (Cai 2017). As of 2018 China had committed over $900 billion in investment along its six land routes and multiple port schemes. At least in conception, the Belt and Road Initiative encompasses countries that contain 65% of global population, 33% of global GDP and 25% of global trade in goods and services. For good and bad it will be a strategic game-changer across many regions that matter to Britain. Or again, between 2011 and 2016 Russia increased the share of its falling GDP spent on its armed forces by over 60% (from 3.4% to 5.6%) even as its economy suffered – a painful strategic shift of national resources. India increased its military spending by almost 10% in successive years between 2014 and 2017, struggling to deal with a stuttering economy and the growth of Chinese military power. Meanwhile, the US defence budget varies from one presidential term to another but still constitutes at least 36% of all world military expenditure. The sheer strategic mismatch between these powers and significant second-rank countries such as Britain, France or Germany is startling. The 'inescapable megatrends' noted earlier would suggest that these strategic shifts are not untypical and can be expected to continue for some decades.

All military and security strategy is ultimately based on national economic strength. That is as true now as it was during the world wars or the Cold War of the previous century. The last thirty years gave powers like Britain a breathing space to exercise some degree of strategic influence, as the fifth biggest economy in the world, while rising powers were working to embrace western-led globalisation. But as the geopolitical wheels turn and globalisation diversifies away from the West, that thirty years may come to seem like an interregnum. Increasingly, the bigger powers define their own strategic relationships bilaterally and those in the second rank try to make their strategic calculations in the diminishing spaces between.

Notes

1   As set out in President Putin's speech to the Duma on 18 March 2014 regarding Ukraine and the annexation of Crimea.

2   COBRA is not a direct acronym. The original ad hoc meetings in 2000 to deal with a strike among petrol tanker drivers, took place in Cabinet Office Briefing Room 'A' – hence the title.

3   The Foreign Office's 'strategy paper' to guide the MoD's 1998 review was produced very late when MoD workstreams were almost complete and was regarded as dysfunctional by MoD officials. It was immediately withdrawn and rewritten inside the Foreign Office by a senior MoD official who happened to be seconded there at the time (private information).

6

Futures: not what they were

FUTURES arrive more quickly these days. When policymakers refer to 'the future' they normally mean those years ahead when they can no longer anticipate what might happen, when 'present trends' will be a shaky basis for further decisions. More than their Cold War predecessors, even more than their immediate predecessors, contemporary British defence policymakers are tormented by the alternative futures they face, and their lack of confidence in the longevity of 'present trends'.

All policy sectors have to grapple with 'the future' in this sense, but defence policy quite acutely. Investments in the heavy metal normally cover a half-century cycle, from conception through to the year when a weapons platform goes out of service, and however agile and flexible are the individuals who operate it, they can only work with what is there. The man or woman who will command the second new British aircraft carrier on its scheduled final voyage will be born around 2020. Defence planners in the second-rank powers are finding that futures arrive far more quickly in the era of globalisation because they can see that those futures are not just politically alternative, but conceptually so too. The structures and rules of world politics are changing rapidly under the technological and economic pressures of globalisation (Bobbitt 2002: 715–75; Ferguson 2017).

The next set of futures, in other words, are not defined as an arc of possibilities from 'favourable' to 'unfavourable' (as they could be in the Cold War) so much as an arc from the 'imaginable' to the 'unimaginable'. Of course, in dire national emergencies societies can mobilise themselves for survival, as outlined in Chapter 1, and do astonishing things quickly. British defence planners have to keep open the means by which this might happen, should the need ever again arise. But they grapple with their tormented futures mainly on the assumption that national mobilisation will not happen, nor will there be more than marginal shifts in governmental resources. The people and the kit they have at any moment will be what they have to address future challenges, however they arise. The 'wars' Britain fights will continue to be 'come as you are' wars.

How well equipped is British defence to face imaginable and unimaginable futures? This is a relative assessment, since all countries face them and those that can cope and adapt more quickly will fare better as the imaginable play out, and the unimaginable take some tangible form. But the mid-rank powers have small margins for strategic error; they are players in the global power arena, not the pillars of it, and their ability to shift large national resources to meet future challenges is constrained.

Assessing Britain's defence qualities

Certain themes have recurred throughout this analysis. One is that Britain is evidently a significant player within the second rank of military powers. Its professional personnel perform extremely well most of the time and operate world-class equipment. Very few countries, even much bigger ones, keep a full-spectrum force structure in being at the expert levels Britain manages. The armed forces gained a great deal of operational experience over recent decades, ranging from fighting two desert wars to rescuing the volunteer arrangements for the London Olympics in 2012. Sometimes the political payoff for military success has been poor; a consequence of flawed overall strategy to which military leadership also contributed. But British forces have not suffered outright military failure in their missions since the Second World

War, and sometimes they have succeeded brilliantly. The world respects their quality and tactical effectiveness.

By maintaining full-spectrum combat forces and keeping defence expenditure above the 2% of GDP required by NATO, Britain also maintained a hefty degree of influence within the Atlantic Alliance, even when it was heavily engaged outside Europe for more than a decade after 2001. In military terms, Britain remains a linchpin of the NATO force structure which links US and European forces in a transatlantic defence arrangement that is still critical to Europe's physical security. With its independent nuclear deterrent, it maintains the fact, albeit as a matter of coincidence, that the five permanent members of the UN Security Council are all leading nuclear weapons states.

It is also true that Britain's ability to coordinate its own policies and to make the most of its full range of diplomatic, military, economic and soft power resources, while not nearly as effective as governments always claim, is still better than in most other countries. In terms of defining and responding to new policy challenges – if not always in resourcing them – Britain is second only to the US (and occasionally ahead of it) in developing national cyber-security, combating terrorism at home, using its considerable intelligence assets, adapting civil technologies to the pursuit of C4ISTAR systems, tracking serious and organised crime, and developing 'smart' foreign aid policy to achieve best political effect. Partner countries across the world frequently take British policy in such areas as a model for their own.

Other themes in this study are less favourable. There is a constant undercurrent of 'overstretch' in all areas of British defence policy. The equipment programme is always ambitious, never entirely funded, and nibbled away around the edges by immediate spending cuts. More effort and resource are put into the desire to field world-class kit than into the people who will operate it – their numbers, their exercises, their general welfare. Their commitment and performance are taken for granted more than that of the kit, which is constantly nurtured and maintained.

Lack of sustainment is another consistent theme. British forces can certainly fight in a war, but they constitute one-shot forces. They cannot be sustained in war-fighting for more than a matter of months; they have to step down to post-conflict operations quite quickly, and even those have proved hard to sustain in more than one place simultaneously. Defence is not all about war-fighting, even if it is the ultimate rationale of the military, but defence planners have also learned that small operations are expensive and can be difficult from which to disengage. They all pressure the fragile sustainability of the force structure.

More fundamentally, maintaining full-spectrum forces for a second-rank power poses the real risk that numbers of deployable troops, ships, tanks and aircraft become so low that they lack *strategic* credibility. They might perform extremely well in operations, but the numbers are too small to make a strategic difference. This really matters to Britain's national defence and security orientation – its highest-level strategy. Britain is, in effect, the 'ten per cent military ally' of the United States. In orders of magnitude, it spends about one-tenth of the US level on defence and gets about one-tenth the size of forces for it. The implicit British assumption over many years has been that this 10% gives Britain some leverage with Washington and some strategic effect on the political outcome of operations, whatever they may be. This was emphatically not to be the case in either Iraq or Afghanistan (Greenstock 2016: 423; Farrell 2017: 422). Those failings jolted the military assessments of Britain's possible future, but had no comparable effect on national grand strategy, which still assumed a meaningful military/strategic partnership between Washington and London. British leaders have always been in danger of mistaking the liking of American chiefs for the British military with their professional judgement of its strategic significance.

Britain also has the capacity to act as a 'framework nation' in organising other allies and partners in operations where the US might not be involved. This is one of the benefits of maintaining full-spectrum forces, since it means that Britain operates military headquarters at both corps and divisional levels, in Combined Air Operations Centres and with full Fleet Headquarters. Few other mid-rank powers do this. That is strategically coherent, but does not necessarily embody strategic *significance*. Strategic significance varies with circumstances, but it is a threshold that forces in small numbers are constantly approaching. British forces fell below it in operations after 2003 and there is more than a suspicion that they may continue to do so.

Another troubling theme that emerges in this analysis is the laissez-faire approach to defence strategy that permeates Whitehall. There has long been an understanding that a whole-of-government approach to defence and security is necessary in the modern world. Defence forces have some role to play in domestic counter-terrorism; top-class intelligence is critical to everything from police forces fighting terrorism to armed forces fighting foreign states; the soft power of information, culture and a society's magnetism should be integrated with the hard power of economic and military policy, and so forth. Britain is good at understanding this and documents its approach in many ways. But government strategy documents are famously abstract, or little more than 'the naming of parts'. And defence strategy documents – the former Annual Statements and latterly the big defence reviews – are locked into a predilection for continuity that is driven by the sheer complexity of defence review processes. The individual services themselves seem to have interpreted the great abstractions of national strategy to suit their own perceptions of the future wars they would prefer to fight.

Above all, what torments British planners and military chiefs alike is the churning fear that they may be preparing for the wrong type of military engagement altogether. The conceptual challenges ahead – the 'unimaginable' parts of the futures equation – hang like a gaseous cloud drifting closer to the foreground (DCDC 2015; Rogers 2016b). Anxiety about new types of warfare – a step change in the *characteristics* of war, as defined in Chapter 3 – come in different forms and at ascending levels of uncertainty.

Western countries can be completely certain that they might have to grapple with 'hybrid warfare' following their own experiences in the Middle East and Afghanistan and in observing Russian behaviour in Georgia, Ukraine, Crimea and Syria over the previous decade. Hybrid warfare refers to campaigns that simultaneously use a wide range of instruments, including distorted information and social media offensives, cyberattack to create confusion, terrorist groups, local militias and irregular troops as proxy fighters, and sometimes also regular troops in formed units but clandestinely and out of uniform (an illegal practice in international law). Other than the phenomenon of social media and cyberattack, there is nothing conceptually new in such hybrid warfare, but western powers have not had to deal with it since the height of the Cold War in the 1950s and 1960s, and some of the West's avowed adversaries, particularly Russia and Iran, have used the technique with some sophistication and effect in recent years. So too, in certain respects, have China and North Korea. Hybrid warfare is certainly a challenge to western defence planners, though it is not difficult to work out how it could be countered, if sufficient resources are available (Kofman and Rojansky 2015).

More uncertain is the prospect of cyber capabilities being used extensively in future conflicts. There is a largely philosophical debate over whether an all-out cyber-war is feasible, where all sides try to disable another's society without using any traditional weapons (Clarke 2010; Rid 2013, Singer and Friedman 2014). In this scenario cyberattack makes living intolerable to the point where a society capitulates to the pressure – creating human misery without violent destruction. Most analysts find it difficult to imagine cyberattacks having the same physical or psychological effects on opponents as violent destruction meted out by either kinetic and non-kinetic weapons. Nevertheless, western defence planners are increasingly alarmed at how vulnerable their own critical national infrastructures (CNIs) have become with the intrinsic digitisation of all industrial control systems. Public utilities, transport, communication links, health provision and government data in most countries are protected by obsolete cyber security. They become networked in ways their own designers no longer understand. Cyberattackers are known to have broken into sensitive military installations in other countries by penetrating the systems operating the street lighting outside them. The fact that Britain's CNI is vulnerable is well understood in government but the depth and extent of its vulnerability remains a matter of conjecture.

Attacks on a country's CNI can certainly form part of a military campaign elsewhere, or a campaign of coercion between one state and another. Such attacks can also be used by terrorist groups to make their point, or by criminal gangs trying to extort money and ransom from big organisations. If 'cyberwars' are hard to imagine, high levels of 'cyber insecurity' are well accepted in all modern societies. North Korea is widely believed to have sponsored criminal hackers whose 'WannaCry' virus, designed to extort ransoms across 150 countries, veered deeply into national health service systems to cause major disruptions in 2017. In 2018 the British government explicitly named Russia as the country behind the crippling 'NotPetya' cyberattack on Ukraine that also caused damage in sixty-four other countries, including Britain. Western intelligence forces are widely believed to have successfully cyberattacked Iran's nuclear centrifuge programme over a number of years using the two versions of the 'Stuxnet' virus, slowing Iran's nuclear programme by some years.

Cyber disruption has already been used to augment a military campaign. Russia used it as part of its short war against Georgia in 2008 and in Ukraine in 2013. It used it in pursuit of political campaigns against Estonia in 2007 and several times against Ukraine after 2013. It also conducted widespread social media offensives across western Europe and the United States to influence elections and exploit any societal disharmony. The uncertainty surrounding cyber elements in modern warfare is that no one can predict where the technology might stop. There is no obvious technological plateau that would limit how disruptive cyberattacks may become and contemporary CNIs cannot reverse their dependence on digitisation.

In their own non-kinetic way, cyber weapons share with nuclear weapons the prospects of endless escalation and huge uncertainty about their aftermath if they were ever fully unleashed. For this reason, western countries have begun to adopt the thinking and strategies of nuclear deterrence as they contemplate cyberattacks. Like the United States, Britain has for some time been able to operate offensive as well as defensive cyber power. It is believed to be one of the best handful of players in the world who can do this. After keeping this capability quiet for a number of years the government began to speak openly about Britain's offensive cyber capabilities in 2011 – a clear indication that, like the *Vanguard* bombers cruising in the Atlantic – it wanted the rest of the world to think in deterrence terms about Britain's own cyber weapons. This may sound reassuring, but nuclear deterrence logic is also an open acceptance of one's own vulnerability and expresses intrinsic uncertainty about the power that might be unleashed.

More unpredictable than all this, however, are the prospects of radical new innovations in many existing technologies, changing the whole balance of effectiveness between modern military forces. Defence planners have only the haziest vision of how far novel technologies might create new forms of warfare that could conceivably invalidate the raw destructive power of the heavy metal, the pervasive influence of 'boots on the ground' to occupy territory, the battle-winning powers of control of the air or low earth orbits, or the advantages of good intelligence, command and control.

The weaponisation of such technologies may not be far away – certainly within the lifespan of many major weapons platforms now entering service. The prospect that current generations of troops could be massively augmented by robotics, artificial intelligence and nanotechnologies is impressive enough; but it is overshadowed by the thought that future generations of troops might be genetically engineered to have particular intellectual or war-fighting advantages born into them. The prospect that current weapons could be made far more accurate to reduce collateral death and damage is overshadowed by the thought that future weapons might be programmed to create new pathogenic characteristics to affect certain genetic groups in a population, or to change the genetic makeup of agriculture or livestock (Kay 2003; van Aken and Hammond 2003). The prospect that the 'computing' element in the C4ISTAR package described in Chapter 3 puts great power in the hands of sophisticated military establishments is overshadowed by the thought that when quantum computing really arrives it may smash all the secure encryption that existing computers can devise and open every computing system, to everyone, all the time (Kaku 2011: 192–5). Secure command and control would go back to word of mouth and written notes.

Above all, quantum computing raises the spectre of binding together combinations of novel technologies, that could link genetics, biotechnology, artificial intelligence, or nanotechnologies to create types of warfare that are beyond our imaginings. Like electricity a century ago, computing is moving from central nodes where it performed a service, to becoming integrated into virtually everything else as a fundamental part of its design. The 'internet of things' is already a reality (Greengard 2015). When it becomes a mature reality, it may possibly change the way current weapon systems operate and which of them remain effective.

Defence planners realise that in the future they may have to compete on all fronts simultaneously; in cyberspace, with information, against artificial intelligence, protecting Britain's critical national infrastructure, guarding against actions which might suddenly devastate the psychological will of the population, or even their physical ability to carry on against genetically-targeted micro-biological attack. The permutations are endless, and the necessary preparations can be no more than sketchy. Beyond thinking about these possibilities, as was commendably done in the study *Future Character of Conflict* (DCDC 2010), how to resource their prevention or mitigation? Realistic options are limited for second-rank powers. Cybertechnology, for example, is the most prominent part of the 'unimaginable' cloud, with dim indications of how cyber challenges might evolve in the next thirty years. Notwithstanding its own vulnerabilities, Britain is regarded as a world leader in cyber security. It launched a national cyber-security policy in 2009. It led many of its partners in 2016 by developing a five-year national cyber-security strategy to which it committed £1.9 billion. But even that represented less than 1% of almost £200 billion that would be spent on mainstream defence policy over the same period. A 1% shift of resources hardly matched the identification of 'cyber threats' as a 'tier one threat to national security' as defined in the National Security Strategy.

This study has emphasised the difference between the nature of warfare and its character. It is fair to conclude that Britain remains good at meeting the challenges that the erstwhile nature of conflict and military operations always pose. The quality, organisation, attitude and commitment to success throughout Britain's defence capabilities are largely undimmed in the post-Cold War world. The future character of conflict, however, is a different matter. It is not clear that a country like Britain can stretch the resources it chooses to make available across the wide spectrum of security challenges that now confront it. Nor would even a doubling of defence resources remove the torment of the planners – though it would certainly make them less jumpy. For Britain, both the imaginable and the unimaginable futures create a fearsome game of risk management with fewer chips and higher stakes than at any time since the Napoleonic Wars.

Alliances and the greatest risks

The best way to deal with high-risk security politics has always been through partnerships, and, in some cases, alliances where states may be committed by treaty to help each other. As one of the pillars of the mid-twentieth-century international order, Britain was an erstwhile joiner of alliances and partnerships, many of which remain effective. By far the most important in the last half century have been the collective defence alliance it has in NATO and the collective security partnership it has in the EU. NATO was overwhelmingly a military alliance; the EU an overwhelmingly civilian partnership. NATO was never very effective when it tried to stray into the political realms of its operations, as it did in Bosnia and Afghanistan, and the EU never managed to create more than a marginal military capability – useful for everything short of organised fighting. But together they represent a good collective synthesis of defence and security capacities in their widest, most modern sense. For all the inevitable strains of maintaining alliances and partnerships between close on thirty states, the combination of hard and soft power they represent, the reinforcement of bilateral relationships and the chance to access technology, research and horizon-scanning among key members, is hard to replicate in other ways. Not least, the NATO part of the combination links the US (as well as Canada and Iceland as geographically important Atlantic powers) to this unique arrangement of states. The eagerness of the post-Soviet countries in central and Eastern Europe to join NATO during the 1990s was precisely to link their future security to the US. Together, the overlapping membership of NATO and the EU easily constitutes the single biggest and most prosperous concentration of liberal democratic countries in the world.

If alliances and partnerships are the best way to confront imaginable and unimaginable risks for mid-rank powers, it is of some importance to appreciate what is happening to them as they affect Britain's situation for the 2020s. In this respect, it appears that a perfect storm has been brewing since the economic crisis of 2008.

First, NATO is in trouble as an alliance. Russian objectives since the 2008 war with Georgia have explicitly been, not to conquer NATO territory, but to neutralise its influence over ex-Soviet states and friends, to lessen the reality of US defence commitments to Europe and create a permissive political climate to the west of Russia that gives Moscow a freer hand to realise the revisionist objectives President Putin set out in 2014 (Neumann 2016). NATO states are openly divided about how seriously to take this challenge and what to do about it. Since

2013 NATO's internal cohesion has been severely strained by Russian bellicosity in the north, refugee crises in the south and the near defection of Turkey from the alliance, working with Russia and Iran against western policy in the Middle East. NATO summits make renewed commitments to collective and effective action, but the underlying trajectory is towards greater allied disharmony (Petersson and Schreer 2018).

Second, the United States is in a long-term reassessment of its role in the world and the extensive global commitments it took on in the 1940s (Haas 2017). The 'America first' slogan of President Trump was not so much a break with the past as an overstated spike in a longer-term trend that can be traced back at least to the early Clinton administration in 1993. Even after the stunning victory to liberate Kuwait in 1991 the US immediately backed away from the commitments that would be required if the lazy rhetoric of a 'new world order' were to be honoured. It would not tolerate US casualties in battle and wanted others to do much more. The 9/11 attacks ended the sensitivity to casualties, but the US was, in any case, in a different mood by 2001. It was clear during the Iraq crisis of 2002 that the US certainly welcomed allies to its side, but did not need them. Secretary of Defense Donald Rumsfeld was happy with 'workarounds' if public opposition in Britain prevented its joining the US. President Obama encouraged an allied air operation in Libya in 2011, but then withdrew US front-line forces to 'lead from behind' – a phrase he hated that dogged his international legacy (Miniter 2012). President Trump exploited the mood but did not create it. In 2018 the Pentagon spoke frequently about the role of alliances in the Trump administration's security policy, but its essential orientation was to unilateral power and action (Pentagon 2018). In a way, President Trump crystallised something that had been happening for a long time (Laderman and Simms 2017). There is a world of difference between a superpower who convenes and leads the group of liberal democracies, and one that invites them to join in courses of action it will take regardless – 'America first' as 'America alone'.

Third, the EU passed the high watermark of its integration and political convergence with the Lisbon Treaty in December 2007. The decade of economic crisis that began almost immediately afterwards exposed big structural problems in the eurozone, which were mitigated but not rectified, set off waves of populist discontent that took both ultra-left and ultra-right-wing forms and created crises of governance in many EU countries (Bouin 2018). A structural migration crisis across Europe added to these pressures, particularly in the southern member states. New barriers went up everywhere and Europe had about the same length of physical barriers across its internal borders as it had during the Cold War, though now in different places (Marshall 2018: 198). All this left the EU with a stark long-term geopolitical choice: reconsolidate and further integrate around a new Franco-German axis, or else accept that the EU would dilute itself across twenty-eight economies that were no longer naturally converging (Webber 2017).

Britain's 2016 'Brexit' referendum vote to leave the organisation occurred in the middle of this EU hiatus, and partly as a result of it. Like the appeasement debates of the 1930s, or the nuclear debates of the 1950s and 1980s – matters of vital national strategy – the Brexit debates will appeal to the judgements of history for any resolution. Leaving the EU is a matter of national strategic orientation which affects many aspects of Britain's global role and the way other countries see it. Whether history finally judges Brexit to be right or wrong for Britain, it will be a decade or more before the first solid strategic conclusions can be drawn.

The perfect storm poses an easily imaginable risk that Britain could find itself strategically isolated in the mid 2020s. In this scenario it proves impossible to contain the aftermath of Brexit to the EU, and it adversely affects Britain's bilateral relations with European partners and thence its role within NATO. The alliance needs to be rejuvenated, but just when this is most necessary Britain's longstanding influence within European NATO may have declined and be displaced by a new Franco-German axis trying to refocus its EU influence into the alliance. The United

States may deepen its scepticism over the value of international institutions and come even more explicitly to regard its allies merely as useful adjuncts, not necessary partners, in enforcing its unilateral interpretation of the rules-based international order. Dealing with a US that may have become entirely transactional with its allies, Britain might find that the lack of genuine strategic significance that its militarily establishment could offer would be cruelly exposed. Between them, the EU and the US (and China) could fall into trade disputes that increase international protectionism, which was, in any case, growing apace after 2008. In this scenario, Britain could find itself both poorer and strategically isolated; its reputation throughout Europe diminished, its standing with the US also reduced for the same reason, and its military forces less useful to Washington than those of allies like Japan, South Korea, some of the Gulf States, and France, Germany or Poland within Europe.

This would not only be a grim prospect in itself for Britain, but would leave it less well placed, with less cash, to address the new types of security challenge that planners suspect are lurking out there. The world is no longer so liberal democratic nor so ordered that a mid-rank democratic power can look after itself, still less pursue the elevated global aspirations that the 1998 defence review set down and which have remained unchanged.

A more optimistic future for Brexit Britain is based on scenarios where the perfect storm has largely passed. If the EU reforms itself to be less centralised, or else becomes more politically diluted by its ongoing crises (including Brexit itself), many of its individual members, particularly in northern, central and eastern Europe, may want stronger bilateral relations with a vigorous, independent military power such as Britain. The aftermath of Brexit, in this view, may have the effect of increasing the priority many European states give to NATO. Correspondingly, Brexit Britain might be more prosperous or anyway make a strategic choice to invest for a decade in its outward-facing virtues to strengthen a 'global Britain' focus – in defence, foreign policy and diplomacy, intelligence, foreign aid and key areas of research and development. This would be an example where resource adjustments might be expected to have a disproportionate strategic impact.

If increasing protectionism does not prevent Britain being a vigorous world trader, and if Britain makes the best of its societal magnetism to attract even more foreign investment, international technology and talent, it might then also be able to use its 'framework nation' military capabilities and be a new sort of '10% partner' with the US – not primarily because it fits into US military operations but because it helps generate other alliances and partnerships that the US values. In northern Europe, the Arctic Atlantic, the Gulf and in the fraught relationships between India and Pakistan, there is ample room for a 'global Britain' to play strategically significant roles within the family of liberal democratic nations and so bolster its own security and prosperity.

A choice of futures

Neither of these futures are satisfactory. The first is unpalatable, the second is unlikely. Muddling through is a natural default reaction, certainly for politicians, if not always for defence and military planners. But muddling through would probably increase the existing vices of British defence policy outlined in this study without augmenting any of the corresponding virtues. Planners always want to keep open as many options as possible when they face the future, hence the 'muddle'. Problems arise where many options turn out to be illusory when tested against real-world requirements.

British defence analysts and planners have become increasingly fascinated by the thought of escaping some of these torments by using technology to jump a generation of force development, moving to very high-tech forces that would deliver defence in different ways – international and holistic 'by design', not as afterthoughts (Gov.UK 2016). The idea of Britain becoming an international leader among the mid-rank military powers in new technology, special forces, intelligence fusion and 'small scale–high effect' operations is an attractive one (Louth and Bronk 2015). It would break away from some of the problems of overstretch and sustainability.

Such an approach, however, would require a big strategic shift (Lawson and Barrons 2016). Britain would spend large amounts of the defence budget differently. It would give up the ability to conduct operations at some scale, it would not truly be operating full-spectrum forces, and its concentration on defence platforms would have to diminish. The dangers of the approach are that keeping alive the structure to handle national mobilisation in the event of major emergencies would be very difficult. Above all, such an approach would depend on a settled view of how Britain's allies and partners, no less than its adversaries, might respond to a country that had even smaller forces but with superpower technologies and an effective way of using them. It would be hard to manage the risks. Nevertheless, faced with an unprecedented range of security challenges – the imaginable and the ever nearer unimaginable – the urge to create better options than currently seem to be available is overwhelming.

In reality, there are unlikely to be any quick fixes on offer without a significant increase in spending on defence, security and key aspects of diplomacy.

The reality is that Brexit has turned medium-term geo-strategic trends that were not going in Britain's favour in any case, into a tipping point for the country; a moment of historical inflexion as significant as the 1840s, 1918 or even 1940. The circumstances of leaving the EU pose something approaching a historical imperative for Britain. If Brexit is to be a strategic success – a reinvigoration of 'global Britain' as the Theresa May government insisted – there will need to be a significant shift of resources into those outward-facing elements described above. British diplomacy, defence policy and the armed forces, the intelligence services, foreign aid policy and governmental R&D together cost around £64 billion per annum, of which defence makes up almost £40 billion. Apart from the absolute size of Britain's £1.9 trillion economy, these are the five key elements by which its existence and role in the world will be judged by its partners. These will be the instruments for it to work to maintain as much of the (favourable) rules-based approach to international order as possible and to keep the country safe and able to make the best of those global economic opportunities that arise.

There is a good argument for a 'strategic surge' – a temporary, decade-long, but significant shift of national resources to make good on the rhetoric governments have used to convince Britain's old (and new) partners that there is a realistic vision of how Brexit Britain will function in an unsympathetic world. In broad terms there is a strong argument to increase defence spending from 2% to 3% of GDP – a 50% absolute increase – for at least five years; to double spending on diplomacy and the soft power assets that support it for up to ten years; and an indefinite doubling or trebling of the £1.3 billion spent by the government on critical and pump-priming R&D.[1] Of course, more resources for certain sectors normally means less for others, and some of the trade-offs against social policy, health or education might be severe if the economy does not grow strongly. Would they be justified? If the present moment is a genuine point of historical inflexion for Britain, and if a strong 'surge' in outward-facing resources could be translated into meaningful policy effects, then such trade-offs would certainly stand comparison with some of those made in previous eras, as mentioned in Chapter 1.

For serious defence analysts, however, a subversive question keeps nagging away. We wonder whether generations of British politicians have consistently failed to address the choices defence planners have offered them; or whether defence planners and military chiefs have simply remained behind the times and carried on 'fighting the last war'. Or perhaps, whether British defence planners are actually ahead of the game among mid-rank powers in realising that it has become impossible for *any* country in this league to offer its citizens the security they expect, given the range of threats and challenges they now face; but they won't admit it to us and have instead become inveterate gamblers.

Note

1   It should be noted that the British private sector spends around £30 billion on R&D and the amount has generally been rising in recent years. Nevertheless, total British R&D spending hovers below 1.5% of GDP and remains far less in both absolute and relative terms than in most of the states it regards as competitors.

Further reading

Bailey, Jonathan et al. eds., 2013, *British Generals in Blair's Wars*, Ashgate, Farnham.

Baylis, John and Kristan Stoddart, 2015, *The British Nuclear Experience: The Roles of Beliefs, Culture and Identity*, Oxford University Press, Oxford.

Brown, David, ed., 2016, *Development of British Defence Policy: Blair, Brown and Beyond*, Routledge, London.

Chalmers, Malcolm, 2018, *Decision Time: The National Security Capability Review 2017–2018 and Defence*, Whitehall Report 1–18, Royal United Services Institute, London.

Childs, Nick, 2012, *Britain's Future Navy*, Pen and Sword, Barnsley.

Dannatt, Richard, 2016, *Boots on the Ground: Britain and Her Army Since 1945*, Profile Books, London.

Defence Concepts and Doctrine Centre, 2014, *Global Strategic Trends – Out to 2045*, 5th edn, Ministry of Defence, London.

Devanny, Joe and Josh Harris, 2014, *The National Security Council: National Security at the Centre of Government*, Institute for Government, London.

Farrell, Theo, 2017, *Unwinnable: Britain's War in Afghanistan 2001–2014*, Bodley Head, London.

Fedorchak, Viktoriya, 2018, *British Air Power: The Doctrinal Path to Jointery*, Bloomsbury, London.

Heidenkamp, Henrik et al., 2014, *The Defence Industrial Triptych: Government as Customer, Sponsor and Regulator*, RUSI, London.

Johnson, Adrian L., ed., 2014, *Wars in Peace: British Military Operations Since 1991*, Royal United Services Institute, London.

Ledwidge, Frank, 2013, *Investment in Blood: The True Costs of Britain's Afghan War*, Yale University Press, New Haven, CT.

Mallinson, Allan, 2009, *The Making of the British Army*, Bantam Press, London.

Porter, Patrick, 2010, 'Why Britain Doesn't Do Grand Strategy', *RUSI Journal* 155(4).

Quinlan, Michael, 2009, *Thinking About Nuclear Weapons: Principles, Problems, Prospects*, Oxford University Press, Oxford.

Ritchie, Nick, 2012, *A Nuclear Weapons-Free World? Britain, Trident and the Challenges Ahead*, Palgrave Macmillan, London.

Self, Robert C., 2010, *British Foreign and Defence Policy Since 1945: Challenges and Dilemmas in a Changing World*, Palgrave Macmillan, London.

Simpson, Emile, 2012, *War from the Ground Up: Twenty-First Century Combat as Politics*, Hurst, London.

Singer, P. W. and Allan Friedman, 2014, *Cybersecurity and Cyberwar: What Everyone Needs to Know*, Oxford University Press, Oxford.

Till, Geoffrey, ed., 2006, *The Development of British Naval Thinking*, Routledge, London.

References

ADS, 2014, 'UK Defence Industry Outlook', *Aerospace, Defence, Security, Space (ADS) Group*, Farnborough.

Aldrich, Richard J., 2010, *GCHQ: The Uncensored Story of Britain's Most Secret Intelligence Agency*, Harper Press, London.

Allison, Graham, 2017, *Destined for War: Can America and China Escape the Thucydides's Trap?* Houghton Mifflin Harcourt, New York.

Arena, M. et al., 2006, 'Why Has the Cost of Navy Ships Risen? A Macroscopic Examination of the Trends in US Naval Ship Costs Over the Past Several Decades'. Santa Monica, CA, RAND Report.

Arena, M. et al., 2008, 'Why Has the Cost of Aircraft Risen? A Macroscopic Examination of the Trends in US Aircraft Costs Over the Past Several Decades'. Santa Monica, CA, RAND Report.

Bailey, Jonathan et al. eds., 2013, *British Generals in Blair's Wars*, Ashgate, Farnham.

Bangert, David, Davies, Neil and Watson, Ryan, 2017, 'Managing Defence Acquisition Cost Growth', *RUSI Journal*, 162(1), February/March.

Baverstock, Neil, 2001, *UK Visions for C4ISTAR and Advanced Technology*, Directorate of Joint Warfare, Ministry of Defence, London.

Beckett, Ian F. W., 2016, *A Guide to British Military History: The Subject and the Sources*, Pen and Sword, Barnsley.

Blair, Tony, 2007, 'A Battle for Global Values', *Foreign Affairs*, 86(1).

Blair, Tony, 2010, *A Journey*, Arrow Books, London.

Bobbitt, Philip, 2002, *The Shield of Achilles: War, Peace and the Course of History*, Allen Lane, London.

Bouin, Olivier, 2018, 'The End of Europe's Integration as We Knew It: A Political Economic Analysis', in Manuel Castells ed., *Europe's Crises*, Polity Press, Cambridge.

Bronk, Justin, 2016, *Maximum Value from the F-35: Harnessing Transformational Fifth-Generation Capabilities for the UK Military*, RUSI Whitehall Report 1–16.

Cabinet Office, 2008, *National Risk Register*, HM Government, Stationery Office, London.

Cabinet Office, 2009, *Cyber Security Strategy of the United Kingdom*, Cm 7642, Stationery Office, London.

Cai, Peter, 2017, *Understanding China's Belt and Road Initiative*, Lowy Institute, Sydney.

Cameron, David, 2015, 'Prime Minister's Statement on National Security Strategy and Strategic Defence and Security Review 2015', *Gov.UK*, 23 November.

Chalmers, Malcolm, 2009, 'Defence Inflation: Myth or Reality?' *RUSI Defence Systems*, 1.

Chalmers, Malcolm, 2015, *The Missing Links in SDSR Financing: Organised Crime, Migration and Diplomacy*, London, RUSI Briefing Paper, September.

Childs, Nick, 2012, *Britain's Future Navy*, Pen and Sword, Barnsley.

Clarke, Michael, 2007, 'Foreign Policy', in Anthony Seldon, *Blair's Britain 1997–2007*, Cambridge University Press, Cambridge.

Clarke, Michael, 2016, 'Planning and Fighting a War: The Iraq Inquiry's Judgements on the Armed Forces', *RUSI Journal* 161(6) December.

Clarke, Richard A., 2010, *Cyber War: The Next Threat to National Security and What to Do About It*, Harper Collins, New York.

Coker, Christopher, 2015, *The Improbable War: China, the United States and the Continuing Logic of Great Power Conflict*, Hurst, London.

Corera, Gordon, 2018, 'Can Mapping Conflict Data Explain, Predict and Prevent Violence?', *BBC News Website*, 16 February.

Dannatt, Richard, 2016, *Boots on the Ground: Britain and Her Army Since 1945*, Profile Books, London.

Davies, Neil et al. 2011, 'Intergenerational Equipment Cost Escalation', *DASA-DESA Economic Working Paper Series*, 1, Ministry of Defence, London.

DCDC [Defence Concepts and Doctrine Centre] 2010, *The Future Character of Conflict*, Ministry of Defence, London.

DCDC 2014, *Global Strategic Trends – Out to 2045,* 5th edition, Ministry of Defence, London.

DCDC 2015, *Future Operating Environment 2035*, Ministry of Defence, London.

DE&S, 2017, *Annual Report and Accounts 2016–17*, HC 534, Ministry of Defence, London.

de la Billiere, Sir Peter, 1992, *Storm Command: A Personal Account of the Gulf War*, Harper Collins, London.

Devanny, Joe and Harris, Josh, 2014, *The National Security Council: National Security at the Centre of Government*, Institute for Government, London.

Diehle, Julia, and Greenberg, Neil, 2016, *Counting the Costs*, King's Centre for Military Health Research, London.

Dorman, Andrew, 2002, *Defence Under Thatcher*, Palgrave, London.

Dorman, Andrew, 2009, *Blair's Successful War: British Military Intervention in Sierra Leone*, Ashgate, Farnham.

Dorman, Andrew et al., 2015, *A Benefit, Not a Burden: The Security, Economic and Strategic Value of Britain's Defence Industry*, London, the Policy Institute at King's.

Economist, 2010, 'Defence Spending in a Time of Austerity', *Briefing*, 26 August.

Economist, 2013, 'No Go, GOCO', 14 December.

Edmunds, Tim, 2014, 'Complexity, Strategy and the National Interest', *International Affairs* 90(3).

Elliott, Christopher L., 2015, *High Command: British Military Leadership in the Iraq and Afghanistan Wars*, Hurst, London.

Farrell, Theo, 2017, *Unwinnable: Britain's War in Afghanistan 2001–2014*, Bodley Head, London.

Fear, N. T. et al. 2010, 'What are the Consequences of Deployment to Iraq and Afghanistan on Mental Health of the UK Armed Forces?', *The Lancet* 375 (9728).

Ferguson, Niall, 2017, *The Square and the Tower: Networks, Hierarchies and the Struggle for Global Power*, Penguin, London.

Foreign and Commonwealth Office, 2013, 'Extremism and Political Instability in North and West Africa', *Parliament.UK*, Session 2013–14.

Francois, Mark, 2017, 'Filling the Ranks: A Report for the Prime Minister on the State of Recruiting into the United Kingdom Armed Forces', July [unpublished].

Freedman, Lawrence, 2008, *A Choice of Enemies: America Confronts the Middle East*, Weidenfeld & Nicolson, London.

Freedman, Lawrence, 2010, 'On War and Choice', *The National Interest*, 107, May/June.

Freedman, Lawrence, 2013, *Strategy: A History*, Oxford University Press, Oxford.

Freedman, Lawrence and Karsh, Efraim, 1993, *The Gulf Conflict 1990–1991: Diplomacy and War in the New World Order*, Princeton University Press, Princeton, NJ.

French White Paper, 2013, *Defence and National Security 2013*, Paris.

Frum, David, 2003, *The Right Man: An Inside Account of the Surprise Presidency of George W. Bush*, Weidenfeld & Nicolson, London.

Gaddis, John Lewis, 2005, *The Cold War*, Penguin, London.

Gaskarth, Jamie, 2015, 'Strategy in a Complex World', *RUSI Journal* 160(6).

Gill, James David, 2014, *Britain and the Bomb: Nuclear Diplomacy 1964–1970*, Stanford University Press, Stanford, CA.

Goodwin, L. et al., 2015, 'Are Common Mental Disorders More Prevalent in the UK Serving Military Compared to the General Working Population?', *Psychological Medicine*, 45(9).

Goodwin, L. et al., 2017, 'Trajectories of Alcohol Use in the UK Military and Associations with Mental Health', *Addictive Behaviors*, 75.

Gov.UK, 2016, 'Innovation Initiative to Bring Future Technology and Ideas to the Armed Forces', 12 August.

Greengard, Samuel, 2015, *The Internet of Things*, MIT Press, Cambridge, MA.

Greenstock, Jeremy, 2016, *Iraq: The Cost of War*, William Heinemann, London.

Haas, Richard, 2017, *A World in Disarray: American Foreign Policy and the Crisis of the Old Order*, Penguin, London.

Hansard 2017, *Parliamentary Debates*, Written Question 111620, 6 November.

Hastings, Max, 2011, *All Hell Let Loose: The World at War 1939–45*, Harper Press, London.

Heidenkamp, Henrik et al., 2014, *The Defence Industrial Triptych: Government as Customer, Sponsor and Regulator*, RUSI, London.

Hennessy, Peter, 2013, *Distilling the Frenzy: Writing the History of One's Own Times*, Biteback Publishing, London.

Hennessy, Peter and Jinks, James, 2015, *The Silent Deep: The Royal Navy Submarine Service Since 1945*, Allen Lane, London.

Heuser, Beatrice, 2010, *The Evolution of Strategy: Thinking War from Antiquity to the Present*, Cambridge University Press, Cambridge.

HM Government, 2014, *Delivering Growth: Implementing the Strategic Vision for the UK Defence Sector*, London.

HM Government, 2018, *National Security Capability Review*, London.

House of Commons Defence Committee [HCDC], 2013, *UK Armed Forces Personnel and the legal Framework for Future Operations*, HC 931, Session 2013–14, House of Commons, London.

House of Commons Defence Committee, 2016, *Shifting the Goalposts? Defence Expenditure and the 2% Pledge*, HC 494, Session 2015–16, House of Commons, London.

House of Commons Defence Committee, 2017a, *Oral Evidence, Work of the Department 2017*, HC 439, 25 October.

House of Commons Defence Committee, 2017b, *Unclear for Take-off? F-35 Procurement*, HC 326, Second Report of Session 2017–19, 12 December.

House of Commons Defence Committee, 2017c, *Who Guards the Guardians? MoD Support for Former and Serving Personnel*, HC 109, Session 2016–17, House of Commons, London.

House of Commons Library, 2012, *The Costs of International Military Operations*, Briefing Note, 5 July.

House of Commons Library, 2015a, *Defence Expenditure (NATO Target) Bill 2015–16*, Briefing Paper 7340, 21 October.

House of Commons Library, 2015b, *The Trident Successor Programme: An Update*, 10 March.

House of Commons Library, 2017a, *Replacing the UK's Nuclear deterrent: Progress of the Dreadnought Class*, Briefing Paper 8010, 19 June.

House of Commons Library, 2017b, *ISIS/Daesh: The Military Response in Iraq and Syria*, Briefing Paper, 6995, 8 March.

House of Lords, 2017, House of Lords / House of Commons Joint Committee on the National Security Strategy, *Conflict, Stability and Security Fund*, HL 105/HC 208, Session 2016–17, 7 February.

IISS, 2017, *Top 15 Defence Budgets 2016 – The Military Balance*, International Institute for Strategic Studies/Routledge, London.

IISS, 2018, *The Military Balance 2018*, International Institute for Strategic Studies/Routledge, London.

Inboden, Will, 2010, 'What's Going on Inside David Cameron's Foreign Policy?' *Foreign Policy Magazine* 2 August.

Ingham, Sarah, 2014, *The Military Covenant: Its Impact on Civil–Military Relations in Britain*, Routledge, London.

Ingram, Paul, 2015, 'UK Nuclear Weapons: A Source of Insecurity?', *Open Security: Conflict and Peacebuilding*, 24 May.

Institute for Fiscal Studies Survey of Public Expenditure in the UK, 2014, IFS Briefing note BN43, London, August.

Johnson, Adrian L., ed., 2014, *Wars in Peace: British Military Operations Since 1991*, Royal United Services Institute, London.

Jones, Peter M. and Reece, Gordon, 1990, *British Public Attitudes to Nuclear Defence*, Macmillan, London.

Kaku, Michio, 2011, *Physics of the Future: The Inventions That Will Transform Our Lives*, Penguin, London.

Kaldor, Mary, 1983, *The Baroque Arsenal*, Abacus, London.

Kaldor, Mary, 1999, *New and Old Wars: Organised Violence in a Global Era*, Stanford University Press, Stanford, CA.

Kaplan, Robert D., 2002, *Warrior Politics: Why Leadership Demands a Pagan Ethos*, Random House, New York.

Kay, David, 2003, 'Genetically Engineered Bioweapons', in Albert H. Teich et al. eds., *AAAS Science and Technology Policy Yearbook 2003*, American Association for the Advancement of Science, New York.

KCMHR, 2010, *King's Centre for Military Health Research: A Fifteen Year Report*, King's College London.

Keegan, John, 1976, *The Face of Battle*, Pimlico, London.

Kennedy, Paul, 1981, *The Realities Behind Diplomacy: Background Influences on British External Policy, 1865–1980*, Allen & Unwin, London.

Kennedy, Paul, 1989, *The Rise and Fall of the Great Powers: Economic Change and Military Conflict from 1500 to 2000*, Fontana Press, London.

Kincade, Bill, 2008, *Changing the Dinosaur's Spots: The Battle to Reform UK Defence Acquisition*, RUSI, London.

Kirkpatrick, David, 2009, 'Acquisition Issues: Lessons from the MoD Major Project Reports', *RUSI Defence Systems*, 1.

Kissinger, Henry, 2014, *World Order: Reflections on the Character of Nations and the Course of War*, Allen Lane, London.

Knight, Roger, 2013, *Britain Against Napoleon: The Organisation of Victory, 1793–1815*, Allen Lane, London.

Kofman, Michael and Rojansky, Matthew, 2015, 'A Closer Look at Russia's "Hybrid War"', *Kenan Cable*, 7, Wilson Center, April.

Laderman, Charlie and Simms, Brendan, 2017, *Donald Trump: The Making of a World View*, Endeavour Press, London.

Laity, Mark, 2008, *Preventing War in Macedonia: Pre-emptive Diplomacy for the 21st Century*, Whitehall Paper 68, Royal United Services Institute, London.

Lawson, Ewan and Barrons, Richard, 2016 'Warfare in the Information Age', *RUSI Journal* 161(5).

Ledwidge, Frank, 2013, *Investment in Blood: The True Costs of Britain's Afghan War*, Yale University Press, New Haven, CT.

Levene, Lord, 2011, *Defence Reform: An Independent Report into the Structure and Management of the Ministry of Defence*, Ministry of Defence, London.

Longford, Paul, 1989, *A Polite and Commercial People: England 1727–1783*, Oxford University Press, Oxford.

Louth, John, 2013, 'It's the Economy, Stupid!', *RUSI Defence Systems 2013*, Royal United Services Institute, London.

Louth, John and Bronk, Justin, 2015, 'Science, Technology and the Generation of the Military Instrument', *RUSI Journal* 160(2).

Macmanus, Deirdre, and Wessely, Simon, 2013, 'Veterans' Mental Health Services in the UK: Are We Headed in the Right Direction?', *Journal of Mental Health* 22(4).

Mallinson, Allan, 2009, *The Making of the British Army*, Bantam Press, London.

Mallinson, Allan, 2017, *Too Important for the Generals: Losing and Winning the First World War*, Bantam Press, London.

Marshall, Tim, 2018, *Divided: Why We're Living in an Age of Walls*, Elliott & Thompson, London.

Melvin, Mungo, 2012, 'Soldiers, Statesmen and Strategy', *RUSI Journal*, 157(1).

Ministry of Defence [MoD], 1996, *Statement on the Defence Estimates 1996*, Cm 3223, London.

Ministry of Defence, 1998, *The Strategic Defence Review*, Cm 3999, London.

Ministry of Defence, 2005, *Defence Industrial Strategy: Defence White Paper*, Cm 6697, December.

Ministry of Defence, 2010, *Strategic Defence and Security Review 2010: Factsheet 2, National Security Risk Assessment*, London.

Ministry of Defence, 2012a, *National Security Through Technology*, Cm 8278, February.

Ministry of Defence, 2012b, *Strategic Communications: The Defence Contribution*, Joint Doctrine Note 1/12, Development, Concepts and Doctrine Centre, Shrivenham.

Ministry of Defence, 2016a, *UK Armed Forces Deaths: Operational Deaths Post World War II*, 31 March.

Ministry of Defence, 2016b, *Quarterly Location Statistics*, November.

Ministry of Defence, 2016c, *Dreadnought Submarine Programme*, Policy Paper, 20 January.

Ministry of Defence, 2017a, *Finance and Economics Annual Bulletin, International Defence 2017*, London, 3 November.

Ministry of Defence, 2017b, *Procurement at MoD*, website accessed 2 January, at www.gov.uk/government/organisations/ministry-of-defence/about/procurement#our-supply-base (last accessed April 2018).

Ministry of Defence, 2017c, *Industry for Defence and a Prosperous Britain: Refreshing Defence Industrial Policy*, London, 20 December.

Ministry of Defence, 2017d, *The Defence Equipment Plan 2016*, London, 27 January.

Ministry of Defence 2017e, *UK Defence in Numbers*, London, September.

Ministry of Defence 2017f, *UK Armed Forces Monthly Service Personnel Statistics*, London, 1 October.

Miniter, Richard, 2012, *Leading from Behind: The Reluctant President and the Advisors Who Decide for Him*, St Martin's Press, New York.

Moore, Darren, 2009, *The Soldier: A History of Courage, Sacrifice and Brotherhood*, Icon, London.

Morgan, Mike, 2008, *The SAS Story*, Sutton Publishing, Stroud.

NatCen 2012, *British Social Attitudes 29, Armed Forces*, NatCen Social Research, London.

National Audit Office, 2000, *Major Projects Report 1999*, HC 613, Session 1999–2000, London, Ministry of Defence, 6 July.

National Audit Office 2006, *Recruitment and Retention in the Armed Forces*, HC 1633–1, Session 2005–06, 3 November, London.

National Audit Office, 2016, *Major Projects Report 2015 and the Equipment Plan 2015 to 2025*, HC 488–1, Session 2015–16, London, Ministry of Defence, 22 October.

National Audit Office, 2017, *Ministry of Defence: The Equipment Plan 2016 to 2026*, HC 914, Session 2016–2017, London, 27 January.

National Audit Office, 2018, *Ministry of Defence: The Equipment Plan 2017 to 2027*, HC 717, Session 2017–2018, London, 30 January.

Neumann, Iver B., 2016, 'Russia's Europe, 1991–2016: Inferiority to Superiority', *International Affairs* 92(6).

NIC, 2017, *Global Trends: Paradox of Progress*, National Intelligence Council, Washington, DC.

Nitschke, Stefan, 2011, 'European C4I and Tactical Communications Update 2011', *Battlespace C4ISTAR Technologies*, 14(4).

Peach, Stuart, 2003, 'It's the Effect That Counts – The Strategic Effect of Air Power', in Peter Gray, ed., *British Air Power*, Stationery Office, London.

Pelling, Henry, 1970, *Britain and the Second World War*, London, Collins /Fontana.

Pentagon, 2018, *Summary of the 2018 National Defense Strategy of the United States of America*, Washington, DC.

Petersson, Magnus and Schreer, Benjamin, 2018, *NATO and the Crisis in the International Order: The Atlantic Alliance and Its Enemies*, Routledge, London.

Porter, Patrick, 2010, 'Why Britain Doesn't Do Grand Strategy', *RUSI Journal* 155(4).

Quinlan, Michael, 2009, *Thinking About Nuclear Weapons: Principles, Problems, Prospects*, Oxford University Press, Oxford.

Quinlan, Michael, 2011, *On Nuclear deterrence: The Correspondence of Sir Michael Quinlan*, compiled by Tanya Ogilvie-White, IISS, London.

Rid, Thomas, 2013, *Cyber War Will Not Take Place*, Hurst, London.

Ritchie, Nick, 2012, *A Nuclear Weapons-Free World? Britain, Trident and the Challenges Ahead*, Palgrave Macmillan, London.

Ritchie, Nick and Ingram, Paul, 2013, *Trident in UK Politics and Public Opinion*, British American Security Information Council Briefing, London, July 2013.

Roberts, Andrew, 2008, *Masters and Commanders: How Roosevelt, Churchill, Marshall and Allenbrooke Won the War in the West*, Allen Lane, London.

Roberts, Peter and Payne, Andrew, 2016, *Intelligence, Surveillance and Reconnaissance in 2013 and Beyond*, RUSI Occasional Paper, London.

Robertson, George, 1999, *Kosovo: An Account of the Crisis*, Ministry of Defence, London.

Rogers, Paul 2016a, 'UK Special Forces: Accountability in Shadow War', *Oxford Research Group Briefing*, 30 March.

Rogers, Paul, 2016b, *Irregular War: ISIS and the New Threat from the Margins*, I. B. Tauris, London.

Rona, Roberto J. et al., 2016, 'Prevalence of PTSD and Other Mental Disorders in UK Service Personnel by Time Since End of Deployment: A Meta Analysis', *BMC Psychiatry*, 16 (333).

Royal British Legion 2009, *Literature Review, UK Veterans and Homelessness*, RBL, London.

RUSI, 2013, 2017, *CDS Annual Christmas Lectures*, at https://rusi.org/event/annual-chief-defence-staff-lecture-2017 (last accessed April 2018).

Shareef, Mohammed, 2017, 'A Paradigm Shift in US–Kurdistan Region of Iraq Relations Post-2014: The Evolution of a Strategic Partnership', in Gareth Stansfield and Mohammed Shareef, eds., *The Kurdish Question Revisited*, Hurst, London.

Shephard, Ben, 2001, *A War of Nerves: Soldiers and Psychiatrists in the Twentieth Century*, Harvard University Press, Cambridge, MA.

Simpson, Emile, 2012, *War from the Ground Up: Twenty-First Century Combat as Politics*, Hurst, London.

Singer, P. W. and Friedman, Allan, 2014, *Cybersecurity and Cyberwar: What Everyone Needs to Know*, Oxford University Press, Oxford.

Sloboda, John, and Abbott, Chris, 2004, 'The "Blair Doctrine" and After: Five Years of Humanitarian Intervention', *Open Democracy Briefing*, 21 April.

Smith, Rupert, 1992, 'The Gulf War: The Land Battle', *RUSI Journal*, 137(1).

Smith, Rupert, 2006, *The Utility of Force: The Art of War in the Modern World*, Penguin, London.

SSRO, 2016, *Annual Report and Accounts, Single Source Regulations Office*, HC 412, 5 July.

Stephens, Philip, 2006, 'High Price of Nuclear Prestige', *Financial Times*, 4 December.

Stocker, Jeremy, 2007, 'A Nuclear Future', in *The United Kingdom and Nuclear Deterrence*, Adelphi Paper 46, International Institute for Strategic Studies, London.

Stockholm International Peace Research Institute [SIPRI], 2017, *Yearbook 2017*, Oxford University Press, Oxford.

Symonds, Matthew 2018 'The New Battlegrounds: Special Report, The Future of War', *The Economist*, 27 January.

Till, Geoffrey, ed., 2006, *The Development of British Naval Thinking*, Routledge, London.

Times, 2018 'Defence Chief is Playing Politics on Spending' *The Times*, 30 January.

Uttley, Matthew R. H. and Wilkinson, Benedict, 2016, 'A Spin of the Wheel? Defence Procurement and Defence Industries in the Brexit Debates', *International Affairs*, 92 (3).

van Aken, Jan, and Hammond, Edward, 2003, 'Genetic Engineering and Biological Weapons', *European Molecular Biology Organisation Reports*, 4.

Webber, Douglas, 2017, 'Can the European Union Survive?', in Desmond Dinan et al. eds., *The European Union in Crisis*, Palgrave, London.

Wessely, Simon, 2013, 'The Psychological Impact of Operations in Iraq: What Has It Been, and What Can We Expect in the Future?', in Jonathan Bailey et al. eds., *British Generals in Blair's Wars*, Ashgate, Farnham.

YouGov UK, 2013, 'Trident: to Keep, Scrap or Downgrade', 15 July, at: https://yougov.co.uk/news/2013/07/15/trident-keep-scrap-or-downgrade (last accessed April 2018).

YouGov UK, 2014, *Report on British Attitudes to Defence, Security and the Armed Forces*, 25 October, at: https://yougov.co.uk/news/2014/10/25/report-british-attitudes-defence-security-and-arme (last accessed April 2018).

Index